Simple Faith

Exchanging Restless Religion for a Restful Relationship

A 30-day devotional journey leading to the simple faith you crave.

KELLIE R. JOHNSON

Keep it Simple!
Kellie Johnson

Scriptures taken from The Holy Bible, New International Version®, NIV® Copyright © 1973, 1978, 1984, 2011 by Biblica, Inc.® Used by permission. All rights reserved worldwide. Scripture quotations marked MSG are taken from *THE MESSAGE*, copyright © 1993, 2002, 2018 by Eugene H. Peterson. Used by permission of NavPress. All rights reserved. Represented by Tyndale House Publishers, Inc.

First paperback edition April 2021

Book design by Bridgette Thompson
Cover art by Jude Beck

ISBN 9798506695349 (paperback)

Published by Kellie R. Johnson
www.kelliejohnson.org

CONTENTS

Your 30-Day Road Map ix

Introduction xi

Part I: Hungry for Change 1
Day 1 Reflection ... What If Fear Didn't Exist? 9
Day 2 Reflection ... Fear vs. Confidence 13
Day 3 Reflection ... Loosen Your Grip 19
Day 4 Reflection ... Just Go Home 25
Day 5 Reflection ... Turn the Page 30
Frame It! 36

Part II: Love God 37
Day 1 Reflection ... Learning to Love
without Limits 49
Day 2 Reflection ... Come Away with Me 55
Day 3 Reflection ... Put Down the Mirror 60
Day 4 Reflection ... His Way Is Love 66
Day 5 Reflection ... Your Time Is Now 69
Frame It! 74

Part III: Love People 75
Day 1 Reflection ... Be Easy on Yourself 87
Day 2 Reflection ... We Are Built for Friendship 92

Day 3 Reflection ... Build a Fire and
They Will Come   97
Day 4 Reflection ... When Sitting
Shoulder to Shoulder Is All You Can Do   101
Day 5 Reflection ... That Time God
Asked Me to Be Carried   106
Frame It!   110

Part IV: Simple Faith   111
Day 1 Reflection ... All In   121
Day 2 Reflection ... Created To BE,
Not To DO   125
Day 3 Reflection ... Be Kind to Yourself   130
Day 4 Reflection ... Keep It Simple Sister   135
Day 5 Reflection ... The Choice Is Yours   140
Frame It!   146

The Wrap-up   148

ACKNOWLEDGMENTS

The courage it took to put this message into a book and present it to the masses was built by life experience and many people who have encouraged me to keep writing. Thank you, Wanda McClure, for mentoring my writing and encouraging me when we began meeting in 2009. That was the start of all of this. To my friend, cheerleader, and part-time life coach, Lynda Young, I am sad you won't see this book come to fruition, but I can see your red pen marks on the pages as you helped make my writing better along the way. To my mama, who read every word I ever blogged until she left for her forever home ... I'm finally doing it. Thank you, Compel Training and She Speaks, and to the countless authors who were willing to share their writing journey so that I could learn and grow.

To my husband, Tim, who spent countless hours on the weekends staying busy so I could sit in my office hunched over the computer. Thank you for your encouragement to keep going and the sacrifice of time together you have so graciously given up for me so I could share this message.

Thank you, my Lord and Friend, Jesus Christ, for pulling back the lens and putting this message in my heart that you have been teaching me over the last 30 years. I am humbled that you would use an average, simple woman like me to point others to You.

SIMPLE FAITH

Exchanging Restless Religion for a Restful Relationship
A 30-day devotional journey leading to the simple faith you crave.

"Teacher, which is the greatest commandment
in the Law?"
Jesus replied: "Love the Lord your God with all your
heart and with all your soul and with all your mind.
This is the first and greatest commandment. And the
second is like it: 'Love your neighbor as yourself.'"
Matthew 22:36–39

The message of Simple Faith is presented here in a simple fashion.

Introduction
This is what you are in for!

Parts
Read these sections as a launching pad for your week. It's the big picture that will be broken down over the next six days into smaller snapshots.

Reflections
There are five reflections, numbered by days, to dive into after each part. It is food for thought and you're encouraged to look up the scriptures that are referenced and reflect on things deeper if you'd like.

Frames
Just as a frame has four sides, you will find four questions to ponder at the end of each week. These thoughts are designed for personal reflection, encouragement, and will challenge you to keep moving forward.

Wrap-up
Here are some final thoughts to bring things into focus.

INTRODUCTION

As women, we tend to long for a simpler time, don't we? I don't know anyone who hasn't at some point watched an episode of *Little House on the Prairie* and secretly dreamed of a life that was as uncomplicated and full of love as what was portrayed on the show. The Ingles family woke up with purpose. There was work to be done and everyone knew their place. They worked hard, staying focused on the mainstays of life like food, water, and shelter. At the end of the day, Ma and Pa gathered around the table with their children, bowed their head to say grace, and satisfied the appetites that had been worked up throughout the day. After dinner, the family would gather around the fire and listen to Pa play the fiddle or harmonica. Their beds called soon after and they enjoyed a quiet night of sleep.

Simple. Focused. Satisfied.

But that is not the world that we live in now, is it? This generation is marked by cell phones, ball game upon ball game, and keeping up with the Joneses. We now have the option to order our groceries online and pick them up in under five minutes (my new favorite thing!). We work hard at jobs that never quite satisfy and come home to a to-do list too long to accomplish before we fall into bed feeling guilty about the things we didn't get done.

Where's the good stuff for us? The deep, meaningful conversation between two friends. The satisfaction of loving God through service that doesn't leave us feeling wrung out week after week.

The technological age that we live in has us so distracted that we are getting some things wrong.

Some of us can't help but compare ourselves to anyone we see doing it *right* on social media. Some of us have been taught that we have to serve others until we can't stand anymore in order to receive man and God's approval. Some of us are so focused on just trying to get it all right that we wind up getting most of it wrong.

When we are getting in our own way, we must
make our way back to God's way.

What if we began to look at placing our faith in Christ as a relief? What if, as we lean in to Him, we realized that we felt more freedom and less burdened. That we were more hopeful and less hopeless. More satisfied and less anxious. Taken care of. Hidden.

When we place our lives in the hands of the Almighty, I believe this is the exchange. His love runs so deep for us that it is not in His nature to make this hard—this relationship with Him. I believe where the struggle lies is in giving Him only part of ourselves while expecting all of Him in return. We give parts while He wants to give us whole. And it can't work this way.

This call to live a life of simple faith really is simple. It's just not always easy. It will bring us freedom and purpose and contentment and so many other things, but it will cost us our entire lives. Our whole hearts. Our traditions. Our man-made rules. Our complicated, religious ideals.

Yes, there is a cost, but the reward is worth it. It. Is. So. Worth. It.

Burnout?

I've seen and experienced wonderful things while being a part of the body of Christ in a local setting, but I've also seen some sad stories play out. See if you find yourself in either of these scenarios:

In an effort to be a "good Christian girl," young Suzie takes on way too many jobs in the church. She comes in to the building, heads for the Sunday school class she is teaching, and then races out to help in the nursery during the main hour. She's back that evening to bring her children to choir practice. Since there aren't enough adults to help there, Suzie takes a seat up front to pitch in where she's needed. Come Wednesday night, she pops in through the side door and bolts right in to teach preschoolers. (After all, her own children are pre-school age so isn't it a *rule* that she has to teach in that department?)

This is her church life. This is where she serves God. Don't get me wrong; her intentions are heart felt and we should all take on some kind of role in our churches, but goodness!

This is a young woman who will begin to believe that her service to the Lord only happens inside the doors of the church. This is a woman whose children are watching her become exhausted with so many jobs that the joy in her service is non-existent. This is a woman who will eventually leave the local church to find some rest for her soul and take some things off her family's schedule. This is a woman who is isolated from other Christian women because her schedule is too full and her energy too low to connect.

This was me for a season.

What about the woman who is a single mom? Sometimes, it's all that Carol can do to get her children to school on time, arrange childcare for the afternoon until she gets home from work, plan a nutritious meal, spend quality time with each child, wash the dishes, bathe the children, say good night prayers with them, and finally fall into bed so she can do it all over again tomorrow.

Carol is a Jesus girl, getting a little Bible reading in during the wee hours of the morning, but she feels like her service to the Lord stops there. No time to serve at the homeless shelter or volunteer for the PTA. There is simply no time or energy left to attend a local church. And spending time with girlfriends? You can forget that!

How can she go to bed at night knowing that she did what she could to point others to Christ? How does she accept the unconditional love that God gives her when she ends her day scrolling through social media only to see that all of the other moms seem to know the secret to getting it all done?

This isn't what Christ intended for us.

There is a better way.

I propose that we've complicated our own faith.

We have taken what was meant to be good and simple and gotten it tangled up in religious practices and unattainable expectations. We've exchanged the uncomplicated life of faith Christ offers us for a life of striving and approval. Of both God and man.

Keep the Main Thing the Main Thing

There is a scene in Matthew 22 where Jesus is the center of talk. The Sadducees and Pharisees had been taking their turns coming at Jesus with question after question. They were trying to trip him up. Disqualify him. The Pharisees, who believed in the full letter of the Old Testament Law, asked Jesus the question, "Teacher, which is the greatest commandment in the Law?"

Sit on this for a moment. Aren't you glad that they asked this question? Don't you want to know what the greatest commandment in the Law is to Jesus? Little did the Pharisees know, but this question was going to be a gift to all who believed in Christ from that point on.

Jesus replied: "Love the Lord your God with all
your heart and with all your soul and with all
your mind."

That's it.

This is the most important command of Christ for all of us.

Love God.
But wait. Jesus went on . . .

> *This is the first and greatest command. And the second is like it: "Love your neighbor as yourself."*

Gift #2. They didn't even ask for the second, most important command, but Jesus gives it anyway.

Love people.
These statements rang out in the street that day. The religious leaders had taken the two things that Christ meant to be simple and twisted them up. They were always observing how people around them behaved and were waiting to see how Jesus would respond. Constantly eyeing. Consistently picking. Boy, some things never change, do they?

These statements from Jesus still ring true today.

Jesus knew the struggles that would come in our lifetime. He knew we needed this. Jesus loves us so much that He dropped this instruction down over 2,000 years ago for us to hang our day-to-day on now. This is the sieve in which we pour our decisions, straining out the unnecessary in order to capture the sweet, concentrated, fulfilled life in Christ. This is the answer to the hustle and grind that we live in, day in and day out.

Jesus loved his Father so much that He gave His life out of obedience to Him. He loved God.

Jesus served us by demonstrating His love for us. He loved His neighbor as Himself.

> *But God demonstrates his own love for us in this:*
> *While we were still sinners, Christ died for us.*
>
> *Romans 5:8*

This is the nail on which we hang our lives in the full security of Christ's own love for us.

My prayer for you as you read each chapter and devotion is that you will take a long, deep breath in your faith journey. That you'll begin to get back to the child like faith you once had ... with full trust and devotion toward Him as you would a perfect father. And that you'll begin to see that loving your neighbor as yourself was never meant to be laborious or burdensome but a source of joy and fulfillment for you.

Lord,

Help us to take a breath and settle our eyes on you. Help us to take what you have given us and make it a priority in our own lives just as you did in yours. To love you first. And to love people second. Help us keep it simple.

In Jesus' name,
Amen

PART I

Hungry for Change

Many years ago, early in my marriage, my husband and I were having some struggles. I was frustrated to say the least. We seemed to be doing everything right. We managed our money pretty well, took our children to church where we served teaching preschoolers. We loved our parents and worked hard at our jobs. But there was still an area where nothing seemed to go just right.

I would pray and pray and journal and pray some more, asking God to take care of this. Why wasn't He moving? What was the hold up? I was young in my faith and had a lot to learn at that point but God lavished His grace on me. He is wise and instead of orchestrating the quick fix that I wanted, He brought about something that would change my perspective permanently.

He exposed something deep down that I didn't know needed work.

He's good at that.

One late evening, I was in the car with a friend of mine running an errand. I began to open up to her about our struggles. When we pulled back into her driveway, she cut off the engine and positioned her body toward mine. She listened patiently as I spilled my guts. The problem, what I was doing about it, and what God *wasn't* doing. I remember the windows beginning to fog and the air feeling damp.

Some of the most meaningful conversations I've ever had were in the car with a close friend.

When I finally stopped talking, she took a breath and looked me in the eye and said, "Are you in love with Jesus?"

What? I was offended she had asked that.

"Of course I love Jesus! What kind of question is that?" Good answer, right?

"No," she responded, "Are you *in* love with Him? Is He your *first* love?"

Whoa.

Not ouch or weird or this is awkward, just … whoa.

I knew immediately what she was asking. What God was asking. I knew that Christ was using this moment to reveal my heart. To peel back the layers to expose what needed to be dealt with. I knew immediately that He was pushing me through a sieve, straining out the fluff and getting right to the point.

He didn't condemn. He gently corrected.

He shifted my gaze from my problem to Him. Eye to eye. For when we are focused on Him, our peripheral vision puts our circumstances in the background. When we are focused on loving Him, on being *in* love with Him, there's not room for much else.

He wants our affection, our allegiance. That's what's most important.

Love People

What wakes you up in the morning, besides the alarm clock? What is it that pulls you out of the bed and causes you to put one foot in front of the other?

Is it your children? Your job? The tasks that if left undone will pile up to overwhelm you so you better just get up and do them?

These are good reasons to get out of bed, don't get me wrong. The problem is that they are also temporary. Our families, our paychecks and our to-do lists will all fade away one day. Some quicker than others.

The second greatest command that is given to us is to love our neighbor as ourselves.

I propose that if we viewed each of these tasks that get us up in the morning *in light of eternity*, we would be more joy-filled as we operate throughout our day. You know that feeling when you lie down at night knowing that all is well and you're actually looking forward to getting up tomorrow and doing it all over again?

Well, maybe you don't. Or maybe you used to and you've forgotten what it feels like.

You see, everything Christ commands us to do is for our own good.

> *And we know that God causes everything to work together for the good of those who love God and are called according to his purpose for them.*

Romans 8:28

Loving others as we would want to be loved is for our good. It's for us!

These tasks that we do each day, they all directly affect others.

Our neighbors.

Our children. Our bosses and co workers. The people in our homes who benefit when we make sure that their clothes have been washed or there is toilet paper in each bathroom. These are all our neighbors. This instruction to love our neighbor as ourselves gives meaning to every little thing we do in our lives that will live on beyond our own existence. This is the stuff that creates our legacy and becomes a part of our story. The story that will be passed on to generations after us.

What would happen if we began to get up every morning with a sense of purpose that would extend beyond our own lives, and we operated in that all day long?

This is where we will experience joy in the menial tasks, those acts of kindness that no one ever sees—like washing the forks that your co workers left in the break-room sink.

This is where we can stay centered and confident when we are folding the clothes or planning the meals or helping a friend who let her car run out of gas. Again.

We were built for relationship. We are better together.

Christ longs to see us in authentic, secure relationships with one another. He desires good in this. He is for us. The more we keep ourselves at a distance from others, the lonelier we will become. The more we hide out in our homes or teach preschoolers on Sundays instead of engaging with people our own age, the more we will become focused on ourselves.

Isolation can be a stepping-stone on the pathway to pride.

When we hold ourselves apart from others, life becomes about us. What feels good to us. What *we* want to do. Where *we* want to go. How *we* want to spend our money. Who will benefit from *our* abilities. *We* decide.

God opposes the proud but gives grace to the humble.

Proverbs 3:34

It's Not about Us

Did you know that there are people who need you in their lives? That only *you* have certain qualities and life experiences that someone else needs to know about or witness firsthand?

Just like you and I need to have other people in our lives, other people need us too!

The scriptures are clear that our own experiences can and will be used to help point others to Christ. He allows some things and wills others all for the purpose of pulling us closer to him and tightening our relationships with one another.

We are wired to need each other and there are people out there who need us. Even if it's uncomfortable hearing that, it's the way we are meant to live. And if we are resisting what we were built for, we are setting ourselves up for a lifetime of unrest and will never experience the deep joy that Christ has for us.

Let's lean in. Let's do this!

When we stay focused on falling in love with Jesus, our day-to-day takes on a purpose that is bigger than we can wrap our minds around.

God can and will do all things. There is a heightened level of peace when we fully grasp the concept that we are not in control, we never were, and never will be. Your faith (when practiced daily) can be earth shaking.

Dave

How We Do It

Change is scary.

Think back to a time in your own life when something took a turn and your knee-jerk reaction was to dig in your heels and refuse to soften the blow on yourself. You stayed stiff and un teachable. After a while, the tension that you build up in your system takes a toll. Squeeze too tight and not only will the rest of your life suffer, but the thing you have a death grip on will eventually cave under the pressure.

Change is necessary.
This simple faith that we want to get back to will require us to loosen up. Leaning in closer to Christ will require us to trust Him fully. And opening the door to relationships will require us to swallow our pride.

Changes are coming.
Let's shift our thinking. Change how we spend our time. Change how we read our Bible. Change how we parent. Change how we show up to work. Change how we relate to our spouse. Change how we relate to strangers.

All of it.
It's for our good. Let's keep that in mind. Anything that God tells us to do is for our good. He is for you.

He is *for* a closer relationship with you. And He is *for* your relationships with others.

Lord,

I want to live in the freedom and security that you offer to me. I want to love you first and foremost while loving others. You know my weaknesses. Help me this week to recognize when fear is trying to lead me. Show me the way to go. I trust you.

In Jesus' name,

Amen

DAY 1 Reflection

WHAT IF FEAR DIDN'T EXIST?

*So do not fear, for I am with you; do not be
dismayed, for I am your God. I will strengthen you
and help you; I will uphold you with my righteous
right hand.*

Isaiah 41:10

What will other parents say? How will my teenager react
to their discipline? How will we pay our bills? What if no
one reads it? What if I don't like it? What if I fail?

I've made many decisions out of fear. Now that I'm
older, it's easy to look back and see the times I froze. I've
kept quiet when I should've spoken up, afraid that no one
would want to hear what I had to say. I've let behaviors
slide with my teenagers, fearing our relationships would
suffer. I've set dreams aside for fear of failure.

Can you relate to any of these? These questions have led me down dark roads in my mind. They've lowered my self-confidence, given me sweaty palms, increased my heart rate, they've fed my self-doubt, and have weighed down my countenance. They're all negative. All rooted in fear.

As believers, this thought process is unhealthy. It's human nature to weigh the pros and cons, but we have to recognize when we are letting our fears of the "what ifs" drive our decision-making. Fear is simply an emotion. One of many that we possess. We need to put it in its place.

I think this is a trust issue.

Plain and simple.

Do we really take God at His word? Are we willing to trust Him in *all* things even if the outcome isn't what we had hoped for?

It's easy to walk in faith when things are going well. When we are claiming His promises to prosper us or bless us. When life seems easy.

But God knew that fear would be an issue.

The Bible tells us "do not fear." It's not a suggestion; it's a direction, a command. I'm a black and white person. I'm glad I don't have to wonder if there is ever an exception. He says, *"Do not."*

Dismayed means to break your courage or become alarmed. You could substitute do not be worried or frightened. Again, there's no gray area here, it says *"Do not."*

Do not fear, break your courage, or become alarmed. He says he will strengthen us and help us. He will uphold us.

What are some of your fears when it comes to loving God first? When it comes to loving others as we contemplate making changes and diving into relationship? I'm sure you have a list. Don't rush through this. Give it some thought.

What would happen if we took fear out of our file drawer of emotions? When we are making a decision, weighing out the pros and cons of a situation, let's let fear walk on by. It *will* walk into our thoughts; we're wired that way. Let's make a conscious decision to not allow it to lead our actions. Take it out of the equation all together.

Imagine what our lives would be like if we did that. Consistently. Daily. We might have less stuff and more resources to give away. We might be raising more respectful children. We might be expanding our families or working our dream job.

What would life be like if we were the first to apologize? If we made the first effort to reconcile? If we spoke up at our PTA meetings? If we chased down that dream we've been harboring since we were young?

This could be life changing. This is part of the freedom that comes with being a child of God.

When we let God guide our decision-making, the end result is out of our hands.

We don't have to second guess ourselves. We don't have to explain ourselves to anybody. I find that so refreshing.

God is looking for people to trust Him. With child like faith. This is where the blessings are. This is where His protection lies. This is where we should be.

Lord,

Thank you, for your word is so clear on this issue of fear. Thank you for providing the assurance that you will strengthen me, help me, and uphold me with your righteous hand when I begin to fear. Change can be scary. Help me to trust you with this.

In Jesus' name,
Amen

DAY 2 Reflection

FEAR VS. CONFIDENCE

*So, do not throw away your confidence; it will be
richly rewarded.*

Hebrews 10:35

Sometimes, when I'm letting my fears hold me back, a
picture pops into my brain. I know I have a fight in front
of me for fear is not from my heavenly father and I've
got to push it away. I must put my gloves on and step in
the ring.

Ever felt this way?

You have a goal. You have a dream. You feel a calling.
But fear has kept you from moving forward.

Here we go, ring the bell ...

Round 1

Fear steps out of its dark corner. Approaching the
center of the ring, its chin held high and its eyes wide
open. Fear

is a champion. It's beat you before. It's wearing a big, shiny gold belt to let you, and everyone else around you, know that it's got your number.

Fear has faced you down before. It knows your weaknesses, your insecurities, your past regrets, your circumstances, and your companions. It has a history of simply walking your way just to see you slink back to your corner.

If you are a Christian, it knows your potential. If your owner is God, it knows your resources. If your trainer is the Holy Spirit, it knows your strength. If your eternal fate has already been sealed, it knows that deep down, you have *nothing* to fear.

But it comes. It tries. It makes an effort. A great effort. Fear is standing between you and your dreams. Your goals. Your calling.

You want to go back to school, but you're afraid you're too old for that.
You want to change careers, but you're afraid of the shift in income.
You want to reconcile with someone, but you're afraid of rejection.
You want to learn to play an instrument, but you're afraid you'll stink.
You want to give to the poor, but you're afraid you can't afford it.
You want to start a business, but you're afraid it will fail.

You want to change your priorities, but the idea of change paralyzes you.

Fear approaches and you run back to your corner of the ring.

Round 2

You've had a moment to catch your breath. Your nerves are on the very edge.

Your trainer has loosened up your shoulders and wiped the sweat off your brow. He's reminded you that you're bigger than your fears. He's reminded you of your previous wins against this very same opponent.

Your owner has already paid a price for you which *guarantees* that you can beat fear.

Guarantees!

What stands on the other side of that fear is something that you cannot even imagine.

What stands on the other side of that fear is a deeper relationship with God.

What stands on the other side of that fear is confidence.

Stand up! Look it in the eye!

Round 3

The bell rings and you've decided to believe what you've been told. You're going to believe that what is waiting on the other side of that fear is something so great, so wonderful, that it's worth the temporary feeling of nausea.

You make up your mind that once your bottom leaves that stool, you're in the match.

No. Going. Back.

Leaving the comfort of your corner, you come out swinging! Spit flying, sweat dripping, heart racing, feet shuffling—all of it!

That's it!

Suddenly you realize that you are the only one left in the ring ...

Kind of anticlimactic huh?

Listen, I've been a Christ follower for a long time, and I am still learning this concept.

> *When we feel a call or have a Christ honoring goal that has gripped our hearts, sometimes all we need to do is MOVE.*

It is that easy.

The Lord honors a willing and obedient heart.

The devil uses fear to keep us from our purpose, to keep us from growing our confidence in Christ.

When we sense a call from God that involves facing a fear, we've got to move. Even if we do it scared. Even if we do it with one eye closed.

And each time we do this, God's faithfulness will grip us with such force and assurance that we will learn to trust Him a little more than we did before.

We'll have experience to draw from.

We'll know that we know that the fear that kept us from striving toward our goal or calling was just a trap to keep us from the plans that Christ has hand drawn for each of us.

confidence
noun con·fi·dence \ˈkän-fə-dən(t)s, -ˌden(t)s\

Simple definition of *confidence*
: a feeling or belief that you can do something well or succeed at something
: a feeling or belief that someone or something is good or has the ability to succeed at something
: the feeling of being certain that something will happen or that something is true

Confidence.

Not in ourselves, but in the One that put that dream in our hearts.

… in the One who is calling us to a deeper relationship with Him.

… in the One that called us out of the corner.

I'm in the ring with fear.

Are you in it too?

Lord,

I admit that fear sometimes keeps me from you. I admit that I am sometimes scared of change. Help me to place my confidence not in my own abilities but in you. In your unchanging word. Thank you that even obedience done in fear, is still obedience.

In Jesus' name,
Amen

Day 3 Reflection

LOOSEN YOUR GRIP

... Do not fear, for I have redeemed you;
I have summoned you by name; you are mine.
When you pass through the waters,
I will be with you;
and when you pass through the rivers,
they will not sweep over you.
When you walk through the fire,
you will not be burned;
the flames will not set you ablaze.

Isaiah 43:1–2

Water is powerful, especially when it comes in the form of a storm.

Lightning. Thunder. Wind. Is it just me, or does it seem that the worst storms come at night? Those tornado warnings or threats of wind damage rear their heads when we can't see what's coming. Adding to the anxieties of the darkness, if the power cuts out and there is little access to news broadcasts, we have a decision to make. Do we take cover, flee, or just shrug our shoulders and go back to bed.

Lightning ... thunder ... wind ... darkness ... these are things that are out of our control.

Sometimes things come along in our lives that create fear and a feeling of helplessness. Maybe it's an illness. An unexpected loss of a loved one. A job loss. A financial need that you have no idea how to take care of. A sick child. An adult child who is going through their own struggles. A relationship that's on the rocks and so on.

There is a story in the Bible about a storm that raged for weeks. The Apostle Paul was on board a ship in that storm and the story of that experience is told in the book of Acts, Chapter 27.

While these men are out to sea, they begin to be slowed down by winds that have set in. The sailing had already become dangerous and then a northeaster wind came and swooped down on them. They had to give way to it. The ship was out of their control and they were forced to go wherever these winds pushed them.

Survival Mode

After two days of hanging on for dear life, they threw ropes into the sea and wrapped them around the ship to try and hold it together. They threw cargo overboard to lighten their load.

On the third day, they threw their tackle over, giving up their ability to fish. They saw no sun or stars for days in that storm.

After fourteen nights had passed, they were still weathering this storm. They were exhausted. They had lost hope. The scriptures say that they were in such a state of "constant suspense" that they had not eaten in all of those days.

Constant Suspense

Have you ever been so pushed around by your circumstances that you felt like you were in a state of *constant suspense*? Your muscles are tight. Your stomach is in a knot. You couldn't eat if you tried. Headaches. Anxiety. All of this together with a feeling of helplessness. You've tried to hold it together the best you could; like these men stringing rope around their ship, you pull in tight whatever you can control.

But rope frays. Its support can only be temporary.

When we are faced with making changes in our lives, don't we tend to hold tight to what we know? What's familiar? We white knuckle and throw our own proverbial rope around what we've held for so long.

Letting Go

The men on that ship tried to hold things together the best that they could. At the same time, they *let things go*. Things that could hinder. Their cargo. Their grain. Toward the end of their journey, they even cut all four of their anchors loose!

There is freedom when we loosen our grip on our stuff. On our old ways. On our old habits.

Oftentimes, God won't take from us what may be holding us in our storm if we are holding on too tightly. He's a gentleman. He won't always pry our little fingers off whatever we have in our hand. Our children, our finances, our marriages, our jobs, our health, our schedules ... let's take a deep breath and loosen our grip a little today. Let's offer up whatever it is that has us in *constant suspense* and everything else that could be keeping us there.

What can you let go of when you need to move? What could be weighing you down and causing you to suffer longer? An item you've gone in debt over that keeps your finances strained? A friend who feeds you negativity every time you talk? Even something that's usually meant for good, like those anchors ... what might you need to cut temporarily to ease the voyage through *your* storm?

Keep Up Your Strength

After two weeks of weathering the storm, Paul urged everyone on board to eat something. To build back their strength.

Women can be especially bad at this. When we are busy trying to take care of everyone else around us, we often neglect our own health. Don't do it. Keep up your strength. Eat healthy, maintain your exercise routine, and continue to make time for yourself. You'll need it all as you shift your priorities. You'll need a clear mind as you step out of your comfort zone.

Once they ate, they tossed the remainder of the food overboard, cut the anchors, untied the ropes, and *drifted* to land.

drift
verb
: to become driven or carried along (as by a current of water, wind, or air) <*a balloon drifting in the wind*>
: to move or float smoothly and effortlessly

They drifted to a land where they were welcomed with fire for warmth and food for nourishment. They were extended the hand of hospitality. There was rest. There was relief. The storm had ended.

Let's *hold together* what we can and *let go* of what we can't. Even if it doesn't make sense in our mind, like those men cutting those anchors, let's let go of anything holding us back from fully loving God and loving others.

Lord,

Thank you for never leaving us. Thank you for keeping me safe and secure as I begin to loosen my grip on what has been so comfortable for so long. Even when it's uncomfortable. Even when it's a little scary.

In Jesus' name,
Amen

Day 4 Reflection

JUST GO HOME

So he got up and went to his father...But while he was still a long way off, his father saw him and was filled with compassion for him; he ran to his son, threw his arms around him and kissed him.

Luke 15:20

Our son was around the age of four. Sitting in the shopping cart in our local Walmart, long legs dangling, he smiled and spoke to every single person within ear shot. Yes, he was friendly then and he is friendly now at twenty-seven.

After hearing him politely ask over and over if he could get down and walk with his dad and me, we reluctantly set him on the ground.

Fast forward three minutes and poof! He was nowhere to be found!

We began calling out his name, scrambling around the department we were in, searching frantically to no avail. I rushed to the front of the store to stop any predators from exiting with him and the store issued their security protocol. Code Adam! All doors were shut and locked and all employees put on alert!

We continued searching for what seemed like an eternity, but in reality was about five minutes, and then, there he was. A stranger who was shopping came towards us with his hand in hers. He had the biggest grin on his face and we had to decide whether to strangle him or squeeze him. We chose the latter.

Our son didn't choose to leave his parents ... he was playing a game. He was hiding in the clothing racks to see if we could find him. We were the one's responsible. *We* had lost *him*.

Jesus used to tell stories, called parables, whereby He would explain things in a manner that were simple, understandable, and relatable.

He tells us in Luke 15 two different stories of things that were lost.

You may be familiar with the first story. A shepherd is tending to his flock. One hundred gloriously dumb sheep. One sheep loses his way while under the shepherd's care and the shepherd leaves the other ninety-nine to search him out. Out of one hundred, only one was lost, and he left the others to seek *him* out. I don't know, but I imagine when he found that sheep, he simply tapped it on the behind with his staff and pointed it in the right direction. Back to safety. Back to a place of security.

The second story tells us how a woman owns ten coins and she loses one in her home. One-tenth of her money. She lights a lamp, sweeps, and cleans her house until she finds it. Once found, she calls her friends over to celebrate. I may steal her idea the next time I lose something!

This next story is an invitation. It's not about a coin or a sheep. It's a person. The only thing that was ever created in the image of God. The thing that God wants to have a relationship with. The thing that has been given free will, to think, plan, and plot, even if it decides to walk away from its creator.

This is you.

This is me.

This man in the story is living with his father and brother. He goes to his dad and asks to have his inheritance early. Like: "I know you're not dead yet, Dad, but can I have my money?"

The father agrees, gives the son his inheritance, and watches him walk out of his life. Through the gate. Off the property. Gone.

Over time, the young man spends every last penny he has. He takes jobs that are nasty and degrading. He contemplates eating the slop the pigs are eating because he is so hungry. He loses his friends. After all, who wants to hang around someone who has no money?

In desperation and humility, he turns to head home. Destitute. Embarrassed. Regretful of his choices.

He knows who will take him back.

From a distance, his father sees him coming home. He meets him with an embrace and a kiss. As his son confesses that he has sinned against his father and God and feels that he is no longer worthy to be called "son," his father reacts with commands to those around him.

Prepare to party! Get my boy some shoes, a coat and jewelry for his hands! Prepare a meal, we are celebrating my son's return!

He does *not* condemn his child. He doesn't issue a consequence. He doesn't scold or embarrass him, he simply loves him. He puts him right back where he belongs, back into the family, not as a servant, but as a blood relative.

This is an invitation for you, for me.

Perhaps you're feeling a little overwhelmed at the prospect of falling in love with Jesus. At the prospect of stepping out of your comfort zone to love others.

Maybe you're like how I was in that car with my friend. Feeling a little like you've missed the mark.

Like the story in Luke, God is watching, waiting, for us to walk back into His loving arms. He's preparing to celebrate as we make our way back to getting our priorities lined up with His.

No condemnation, only love.

Take your hand off the gate.

Step back inside the fence.

Turn back toward Him.

He is waiting eagerly for your return.

Just go home.

Lord,

I am tired of doing things my way. I am tired of doing what religion and tradition tell me if you're not in it. If you're not the center. I'm coming back to my first love today. Thank you for patiently waiting on me.

In Jesus' name,
Amen

Day 5 Reflection

TURN THE PAGE

Choosing to Trust the Author of Our Stories in the Midst of Hard Chapters

By no means do I count myself an expert in all of this, but I've got my eye on the goal, where God is beckoning us onward—to Jesus. I'm off and running, and I'm not turning back.

Philippians 3:13–14 (The Message)

I recently took a day to put the top down and take some back roads. I love taking in the sights of small-town America and imagining how those towns first came to be. Who settled there first, and who keeps the livelihood going. I love old buildings and dirt roads and sunflower fields ... all of it. It fills me up spiritually and I'm able to reflect on those moments and draw inspiration from those places.

I imagine those first generations that came in and settled had a hard time. They had to endure financial barriers and sickness, planting and harvesting on new soil, and just flat-out fatigue. I wonder if they were ever tempted to close the book on their lives and be done. I wonder what kept them going and inspired them to keep turning the pages and moving on in the stories that they were a part of.

These people were working for something better. They were building a future for their children and their children's children. They were creating changes on their own and having to endure changes that came with the wind.

Change.
It's inevitable and it's annoying and it's beautiful and inconvenient; it's stressful and it's welcoming and it's unwelcome and it's scary.

Oftentimes, changes will take place in our lives that we have *no* control over. The flip side is that there are some changes that *need* to come into our lives in which we have a choice about.

This is where it can get sticky.

We may not always like the choices that lie before us. Sometimes we don't even know what choices we have as we have to close a door behind us before we can turn to look at the other doors before us. Does that make sense?

I believe oftentimes a choice stands before us, one we may not even see yet, and God is waiting for us to simply wet our fingers, reach out, even if with eyes closed, and turn the page.

No one is an expert, just move onward. Run ... no turning back!

A sweet friend of mine frequently says, "God is writing my story."

Think of your life as a book. It's unique and beautiful on its own. Like any good story there is joy and sadness. Suspense and intrigue. New characters are introduced and old ones leave. There are stories within the story. Battles fought, some wins, some losses, always a lesson learned.

But the ending. This is where turning the page will get you. You *have* to turn the page to get to the ending.

The ending is where the good stuff is. Where the author takes all of the pieces of our story and ties them together for a finish that we could never have imagined.

That *doesn't* mean it always appears to be a happy ending in *our* eyes. But, it *does* mean that the Author is pleased with the finished product. That the masterpiece He created, which is YOU (and me), is complete.

Our lives, our stories, aren't to be tucked away on a shelf to collect dust and stay hidden from the world. They're a testament to the Author. They are a word-of-mouth endorsement for others to take interest in and see the work of God and the hope that living a life for Him brings. Even during the moments of the unknown, suspense and sadness, if it's too much to read that chapter out loud as it's being written, share it with others once the page has been turned and you have the gift of hindsight to go along with that part of your story.

> *God can stun you in hindsight when you discover the careful orchestration of events in your life.*
>
> *Priscilla Shirer*

Remember, those hard times are only a part of you, not the whole. Every story intertwines the good with the bad. You are no exception. But you and I get to choose whether we are going to park ourselves on the negative or just glance there and set our gaze on the positive.

I've seen what this Author can do with a willing participant. I've read His other works that are scattered throughout history (HIS-story). I've seen friends and family make hard decisions that they *never* regretted. But ask them about the choosing, and they'll tell you that in the flesh, it wasn't always easy.

Some days I'm still learning to keep moving and trust. To turn the page even when I'm afraid of what may be on the other side. If you feel this way, you are not alone. This has been going on from generation to generation.

I imagine the people who settled on these lands first had to make hard choices and they had to make them quick. They didn't always have the luxury to watch a fever for a few days before making the trek to the doctor's office. They couldn't watch their crops be swarmed by locust and spend a few weeks contemplating whether they should burn or just stand by and wait and see. They had to move quickly, making split-second decisions, not always knowing what the outcome would be for their families as they flipped the pages in their lives.

Look around at how far these little towns have come. You're living in one now. We have the people who were here first to thank for that. They kept turning the pages in their lives, moving forward, building something for the rest of us to reflect on and be thankful for and continue building from.

When we are given choices, it's a gift.
Even though making a choice can be excruciating, if we stand by paralyzed with fear, we will grow stiff. Cold. Our stories can become uninviting for others who want to be a part of our lives.

You've been given a choice. Stay on the page you are sitting where dust will collect and the beauty of the words will soon fade, or perhaps reach out with your other hand to do the turning. Maybe you need a friend to come alongside and help you turn your page. Perhaps you need to pick up the book, shake it out and attack that page turning like you never have before.

God is writing your story.
It's not over yet. The momentum is building and there may be people around you just biting their lip to see what the next chapter of your life holds. They aren't fixated on *you*,

they're looking to the *Author*. They've read His stories before and they know that He never disappoints. Never.

Lord,

Thank you that even though I'm a little intimidated about leaning in to you while embracing others, I can trust you. Thank you for putting people in my life whom I can watch and learn from as they keep their focus on you. If I am lacking in this, I would ask you to provide those examples for me. I'm ready to turn the page.

In Jesus' name,
Amen

FRAME It!

1. As you embark on making changes in your life, is there anything you are afraid of?

2. If you feel you were ever taught to value religious practices over a relationship with Jesus, take a few moments and search your heart. Perhaps you need to forgive someone, or even yourself, in a moment of solitude.

3. As you shift your mindset from religious thoughts to relational thoughts, you'll begin to feel a change in your spirit. Jesus tells us in Matthew 11:28, "Come to Me, all you who are weary and burdened, and I will give you rest." Take a few moments and thank Him for bearing the burdens you have been carrying.

4. What's one change you know is already taking place in your spirit as you have focused on making small changes to your faith life? This is called transformation.

Do not conform to the pattern of this world, but be transformed by the renewing of your mind.

Romans 12:2a

PART II

Love God

*"Teacher, which is the greatest commandment
in the Law?"
Jesus replied: "Love the Lord your God with
all your heart and with all your soul and with
all your mind. This is the first and greatest
commandment."*

Matthew 22:36–37

What Is It?

How do you know that God loves you?-

*"The Bible tells me so!" But really—the relationship is loving,
He spends time with me and I with Him. On the days I don't love
myself, especially on those days, He reminds me how loved I am.*

Mimi

Love.

What do you think of when you hear the word "love" or even use it yourself? Some might say it's a word that we over use. What I know is that it's only four letters long and it spans from the very beginning of everything into eternity.

Christ defines it for us.

> *Love is patient, love is kind. It does not envy,*
> *it does not boast, it is not proud. It does not*
> *dishonor others, it is not self-seeking, it is not*
> *easily angered, it keeps no record of wrongs. Love*
> *does not delight in evil but rejoices with the truth.*
> *It always protects, always trusts, always hopes,*
> *always perseveres. Love never fails.*
>
> *I Corinthians 13: 4–8*

Whoa! A pretty exhaustive description, right? But, one we can sink our teeth into. Aren't you glad He spells it out for us?

I see a few things here, so let's break it down.

Love is...

Patient, long-suffering,
Kind, thoughtful, attentive.

Love does not...

envy
boast
dishonor others
keep records of wrongs
delight in evil but rejoices with the truth.

It is not...
self-seeking
easily angered
proud.

Love always...
protects
trusts
hopes
perseveres.

Love never fails.

As we break down this scripture, I am struck at how most of it points to the area above our neck. Our minds.

Love doesn't demand that we wear ourselves out or we jump through hoops or try to climb up to God's level. Love doesn't dictate what we wear or where we work or any of that. Love is a mindset. An attitude. Love sets up guardrails in our minds that keep us on track and moving forward.

The beauty in loving God with all our heart, soul and mind is that we don't have to stretch up to catch His eye, but that He has stooped down to meet us right where we are.

This is Jesus.

He embodies love. He *is* love. He has set the example and loved us first. Not only did he instruct us, but He provided a living example in himself.

That exhaustive list in I Corinthians that we just read—what love *is*, what it *is not*, what it *does not*, what it *always does* — Christ didn't simply express those things, he *is* those things. And as an expression of those things, Jesus lived his life according to the scriptures, according to what he asks us to do, which is to love him fully.

He loved *us* fully. Not partly or almost thoroughly, but completely. He literally completed the task of demonstrating his love for us when he was put to death. When he obeyed his father and walked through the valley of the shadow of death all the way to Mount Calvary. When he breathed his very last breath, he sealed the deal on his love for us, for once the physical body passes, it cannot undo what's been done. A final breath. One final expression of the love of Christ. And as Jesus breathed his last, the veil was torn and the ability to have a one-on-one relationship with God became a reality. The thing that Christ wanted for so long had finally come into fruition. For now, mankind could have intimacy with their creator, and love him like Jesus did.

Avail yourself of the greatest privilege this side of heaven. Jesus Christ died to make this communion and communication with the Father possible.
Billy Graham

Love never fails. Never.

A Daunting Task

When our children were small, we took a lot of trips to the park. Any kind of outdoor activity was time well spent.

While their small stature kept their eyes focused on what was low, they took interest in small things. Things their little hands could grasp.

Rocks, sticks, wildflowers, and leaves were among the objects we would touch and feel and talk about. "Who created that leaf? Didn't God give us beautiful things to enjoy?" I would often ask.

But on occasion, we would happen upon large trees. The kids would attempt to wrap their arms around those massive tree trunks. They'd get on their tippy toes and look up as if searching for a better place to grasp. At times, they would even place themselves opposite one another and reach in an attempt to touch their fingers together on either side. I guess if they could do that, they would feel successful in their tree-hugging attempts.

When scripture tells us to "love God," do you ever feel as if it's just too big a task? Does it seem impossible to wrap your minds around what that would look like? And like my young children, have you ever written it off as an impossible task only to walk away and stay focused on what was easy and more within your reach.

I've been there. When it seems that I am loving God, but I can't feel His love reciprocated. When it feels like the task is the size of an elephant and taking small bites out of the job won't get me far. I've stood on my proverbial tippy toes and reached up as far as I could only to feel as if His gaze is so far over me that surely, He doesn't even know I'm down here.

Scripture is clear that we are to love God. Not only love Him, but to do so with all our heart, all our soul and all our mind. Every cell, every breath, every step, every word, every thought.

Father, Papa, Daddy

In 2016 the Census Bureau reported that nearly one-fourth of the population of children in America were living only with their mothers. That doesn't include children living with grandparents or in the government system without any parents at all. It doesn't include children being raised by other relatives or those staying with friends because things were too hard at home.

Friends, that's a lot of missing fathers. That's a lot of children without daily contact with a parent.

Maybe you yourself grew up in a home where your father was absent. Perhaps he was close by, but the day-to-day business of life didn't include him. No discipline for the first speeding ticket you got. No sideways grin when he caught you pulling the wool over your mother's eyes. No instruction on how to change your oil or a flat tire. He wasn't walking in the door each evening after work, eager to hear about your day.

There is a longing in each of us for these experiences with our father.

That relationship that we long for can be found in loving Jesus. Correction. It can *only* be found in Jesus. Even if you were brought up with a loving father or father figure in your home, that man is still just a man. They have the ability to reflect the love of God onto their children, but a reflection is not a substitute for a relationship with God Himself.

That desire to please our earthly father points us to our true Father in heaven.

That desire to know what our father thinks is best for us, points us to asking Christ what we should do.

That desire to be held by our father when we are broken beckons us to curl up in the presence of our heavenly father.

He is our source of confidence, wisdom and comfort. *The* source.

Each time we run to Him with our questions and our celebrations, it is an opportunity to grow closer to God. It's one of the many ways that we demonstrate our love for Christ. We make Him our first love. The object of our affection and the One whom we place our total trust in.

This is love.

What's the Big Deal?

Think of someone that you love. Someone that you love with all your heart. Maybe it's your spouse. Maybe it's your child. Maybe both. Perhaps it's a lifelong friend or even a parent.

These people that we love, do we know how to love them well? If they are important to us, we will figure it out, won't we?

What *do* you like?

I've got a close friend who likes chocolate. When she's going through a tough time at work or is struggling with something, I'll grab her a little chocolate, wrap it in some pretty tissue paper and hand it to her when I see her. It costs so little but means so much!

My husband loves a certain coffee from a certain little coffee shop. If I'm out near that shop or I've met a friend there for my own cup of coffee, I'll grab him one and bring it home to him. You should see his eyes light up when I hand him that cup!

One of my mom's love languages right now is time. No need for gifts or tokens, just time spent together. Because I love her, I make time to see her. And I don't just squeeze her in, I intentionally plan when we can be together and not be rushed. We may run to a local antique store or it may even be that I've offered to take her to a doctor's appointment, but we are together, and she loves it (me too), and in doing this, she doesn't have to doubt my love for her.

When we love someone, we find out what's important to them. What makes their eyes light up. What grabs their attention. What is it that helps that person to know how we feel about them without saying a word.

This is one way that we love God. We get in His word and find out what's important to Him. Find out what grabs His attention. Then we do the thing! His word is rich with stories and directives pointing us to what has His heart. We just need to dig in and stay there. It won't take long to figure it out.

Make much of me

In today's culture, we scroll through social media to see the highlights of everyone's life, even the people we never see in person. As a mom of young adult children, if I see that another mom on my media feed has been called out and bragged on by their child, I stop and read. Because I can relate to the position in life that she is in, I can also relate to how special it feels to have your child speak kind of you publicly.

Have you ever been in a group conversation and heard other women speak of their husbands respectfully? The husbands aren't even within ear shot and yet the women are boasting about what a great partner they have when it comes to raising their children or keeping the laundry train running. Maybe someone's husband is a hard worker and so she makes a point to mention that she is proud of his work ethic.

Maybe you've been in the opposite situation. You're with other women and suddenly one begins to make snide remarks about her husband. Have you ever wanted to stand up and take up for him? Defend him?

Maybe it's a friend of yours that's falsely accused. Just a small deviation from a story in their life being told by a third party and things can get out of control quickly. Do you speak up and shut it down? Yes! You know this friend intimately and you can speak on their behalf. You have some power over protecting their reputation and so it comes naturally to react this way.

When we love someone, we want to make much of them. We point them out to others with a grin on our face and pride in our heart that we actually *know* this person. Any time we point others to Christ, it's an expression of our love for Him. An expression of our trust in Him that is solid enough to recommend a relationship with Him to everyone else.

Then there's the opposite side of that. If we hear someone bash our heavenly father, if we love Him, we will take up for Him. We will speak out of our own experiences with Him and stop any misinformation from spreading. This is another expression of our love for Him.

Come Away with Me

Jesus often withdrew to lonely places and prayed.

Luke 5:16

These people that we love so dear, more than anything, we want to spend time with them. There is nothing better than sitting in a little coffee shop with your best girlfriend sharing your life over a hot cup of something, am I right? What about those overnight get-aways with your spouse? After raising the children and working the jobs and going on double dates, time with just the two of you is really where the sweet stuff is found. Rest. Authentic conversation. Secrets.

Jesus often got away to spend time with His father. He had exceptionally long days filled with hundreds of people constantly crowding him, always wanting something. He was tired. He was possibly tired of talking. But He made the time, even if it meant losing sleep. Even if it meant missing a meal or having outsiders wonder what in the world He was doing. There was important work to be done after all, why would Jesus keep skirting away, alone, to pray?

His Father was His source. His provision, His direction, His rest when He was tired … His everything.

He is ours too. We can brag about Him, we can stand up for Him, we can find out what it is that He is passionate about and take part in making a difference, but if we aren't taking time out to spend one-on-one time with Him, it will all be for naught. This is our great expression of love. Giving Him our time and attention, on a daily basis. If we do this, everything else will fall right into place.

> *Seek first his kingdom and his righteousness, and*
> *all these things will be given to you as well.*

> *Matthew 6:33*

This is our starting point to a simpler faith. Loving God.
Simply.

Lord,

I want to love you well. Teach me in your Word. Show me
what's important to you. I'm grateful for you, who you are,
what you've done for me and will continue to do in the future.

In Jesus' name,
Amen

Day **1** Reflection

LEARNING TO LOVE WITHOUT LIMITS

In the first book of Peter, Peter is writing, instructing the church on a number of things. Dos and don'ts. How to live a holy life. Warnings on avoiding sin and so on.

Toward the end of the book, he seems to wrap up all those details with this...

> *Above all, love each other deeply, because love covers over a multitude of sins.*

1 Peter 4:8

God knows that even though He can *tell* us how to live, He can *show* us how to live and He can *motivate* us on why we should live in this way ... we need simple.

And there is nothing more simple than loving someone.

*I lost some of you there, didn't I? We've all had
someone we tried to love and it just seemed difficult. May I suggest it was not loving them that
was difficult, but in our expectations of their reaction to our love that made it so? God doesn't ask
us to love according to how the other person will
respond. He just tells us to love. Unconditionally.
Like His love for us.*

Why should we love without limits?

God's love for us is the thread that is woven throughout
scripture. Every story. Every word. It all boils down to His
love for us.

Before our very existence, we were loved. Unconditionally. Out of our own experience of being loved without
any strings attached, we love others. Taking what has been
freely given to us and passing it on. Good stuff in, good
stuff out.

*But God demonstrates his own love for us in this:
While we were still sinners, Christ died for us.*

Romans 5:8

In light of what Jesus has done for us, who are we to withhold our love from others?

Indulge me for a moment and allow me to string some
words together that I see in the good Book. I'll reference
where they are if you'd like to look at them in context.

If you love those who love you, what credit is that to you? Even sinners love those who love them.

Luke 6:32

Above all, love each other deeply.
1 Peter 4:8a

"...Love covers over a multitude of sins."
1 Peter 4:8b

"...love never fails."
1 Corinthians 13:8a

Love *never* fails? Doesn't that mean that it *always* wins? That's good news!

Who do we love without limits?

Everyone.

The second is this: "Love your neighbor as yourself."

Mark 12:31a

Who is it that you have a hard time loving?

That neighbor who comes and goes at all hours?

That boss who takes advantage of his/her flexible schedule?

That new friend of your child you just don't like?

That family member who keeps disappointing you?

That ex-spouse who won't pay their child support?

That father that walked out when you were a child?

That counselor who keeps giving you homework in your marriage?

That teacher who plays favorites in your child's classroom?

That person staring back at you in the mirror every morning?

No one is exempt. No one has used their sin card too many times. No one is so despicable or deplorable that we are not to love them. God doesn't withhold His love from anyone, and we are to follow His lead.

How do we love without limits?
He makes this so easy for us that He even defines what love is.

> *Love is patient, love is kind. It does not envy,*
> *it does not boast, it is not proud. It does not*
> *dishonor others, it is not self-seeking, it is not easily*
> *angered, it keeps no record of wrongs. Love does not*
> *delight in evil but rejoices with the truth.*
> *It always protects, always trusts, always hopes,*
> *always perseveres. Love never fails.*

1 Corinthians 13:4–8a

> *It keeps no record of wrongs.*
> *It does not dishonor others.*

Ouch.

As believers in Christ, we are to be conduits. A pipeline of sorts.

Think of a storm drain. The fresh, clean rains pour down and those drains have the task of funneling that water from one place into another. Sometimes they get clogged with trash and muck. When they do, the pipes can't do what they were made for. Water backs up.

The source of the water keeps pouring in and the pipe becomes stressed and bloated. The water that was supposed to run through is now sitting, attracting insects, and becoming stagnant. On the flip side, the areas that desperately needed that water are left thirsty. Soil sits dry. Pipes begin to age and crack.

The love Christ has poured into us...let's be careful not to slow down that flow with a bunch of trash in our pipes. Trash like pride, anger, jealousy...

I've had a name or two on a list before. People I did *not* want to even *think* about loving. Content to let someone else throw them a smile or be kind. Holding wrongs against them seemed, and seems, like the intelligent thing to do, right? Aren't we supposed to judge people by their fruit? Yes.

But just because I love someone, doesn't mean they are my new best friend. It doesn't mean I agree with their choices or we need to start meeting for coffee.

Loving them simply means that I recognize that I am no better than they are in the sight of the One who gives us both breath. We are on a level playing field. There is only one Judge and I am not it.

I'm learning that I can love someone up close and I can love someone from a distance. I'm learning that people are in my life on purpose, for a purpose. I'm learning that while I learn to love, even when I don't want to, it changes me. I become less self-centered and more thankful for the grace that God extends to me every single day.

He loves. I love. It will never fail.

I'm learning a lot about this and it's all good.

Why do we love without limits?

Because we are loved without limits.

Who do we love without limits?

Anyone with breath in their lungs.

How do we love without limits?

With perseverance and constant hope.

Lord,

The love you have for me is incomprehensible. I cannot understand it all. I cannot categorize it or package it in a way that makes complete sense. But I accept it. And I want to love others without limits, just as you love me. Thank you for entrusting me with the love you have for others. Help me to demonstrate my love for you in a way that honors you and draws others into fellowship with you.

In Jesus' name,
Amen

look
th

Day 2 Reflection

COME AWAY WITH ME

Years ago, I was involved in a study that focused on spiritual disciplines. My kids were small and life was busy but once a week my husband and I met with a few other couples to do this. The end of the study culminated in taking a half day away just to pray.

Four hours.

We spent four hours at a beautiful local park. I sat near the lake. Spent time near a covered bridge. Cozied up to a tree with a view of a water wheel. Notebook. Bible. Water. Pen. That's all I needed.

It was marvelous!

Nature is a powerful thing.

There's something about being out in nature that soothes the soul. Would you agree? Wind, birds, squirrels, butterflies. You notice the little trail of ants carrying their food from place to place. How the trees can take on a different the sun shines from a different angle throughout the day. How the clouds change shape as they skim across the blue sky effortlessly. The wind relaxes and the muscles let go of their tightened state.

Something happens when we get outside, to a lonely place, and just look about. His power becomes more evident. His creativity shines everywhere you look. His attention to detail. All of it is a reminder of what a great big God we serve. All of it!

Jesus prayed often.

Even to say that seems like an understatement. But there were times that He had to break away from the noise and get to a quiet place. Doesn't that sound marvelous?

Be alone to talk.

Be alone to listen.

Just be.

> *Jesus often withdrew to lonely places and prayed.*
>
> *Luke 5:16*

I see three important truths in this verse that we can take in and flesh out.

Jesus withdrew.

He drew away from the pressures of His life, detached Himself, became removed

He did it often.

He did it frequently, repeatedly, and consistently. He made it a habit. A lifestyle.

He chose lonely places.

He struck out unaccompanied. He went solo. He isolated Himself.

If this was a part of Jesus' lifestyle, I'd say that we should incorporate this practice into our own lives. Especially in the world that we are living in that is so inundated with noise and movement and visual stimulation everywhere you look.

I need this. You need this.

- High school or middle school student who attends church each week but doesn't really know how to pray.
- College student who studies the Bible in their dorm room each day while listening to nearby students crank their music and holler down the hallway.
- Young mama who can't even use the bathroom without interruption.
- Mom of teens whose door revolves around your kids and their friends.
- Empty nesters who aren't quite used to the sound of an empty house.
- Retired older woman who putzes around all day trying to keep herself busy.

Ladies, some of us seem to need permission to get away by ourselves, for even just a couple of hours. This is it. This is your permission, encouragement and your convincing argument that you *must, we* must, make this a practice.

It was important to Jesus. And it's just what you do when you love someone. You spend quality time with them.

It should be important for us.

And I believe that it will not only benefit our relationship with God, but it will ultimately benefit our family, our work, our church, and all the other parts of our lives.

Let's get out our calendars and mark a date or two to get started. Pick a nearby place—away from home—grab your Bible and a coffee and keep that appointment. There is nothing as important as keeping that line of communication with God open and active.

This could be the thing to take your walk with Him deeper than it's ever been.

This could be the thing you need to hit re start on your relationship with Him.

If you need some help getting started with your prayers, here's a simple way to think about it.

P.R.A.Y.

Praise! Begin your conversation with your Heavenly Father by praising Him. It takes the focus off ourselves and puts it on Him. It begins a vertical conversation. It recognizes that He is in a position of honor and respect.

Repent! I John 1:9 says, *"If we confess our sins, he is faithful and just and will forgive us our sins and purify us from all unrighteousness."* After we've lifted praises to Him, take some time to ask Him to bring any sin to mind that you need to ask forgiveness for. He will be faithful to forgive.

Ask! Once you've taken the time to praise Him and start with a clean slate, ask Him for the things that you need. Ask for yourself as well as any other needs that are on your heart.

Yield! No matter what you've talked to the Lord about, ultimately, you need to yield your own will to His. He knows more. He knows best. He knows it all! As Jesus prayed right before His crucifixion, He Himself said in Matthew 26:39 *"My Father, if it is possible, may this cup be taken from me. Yet not as I will, but as you will."* He is a good, good father and He knows what is best for us. Trust that.

Lord,

I want to get to know you more. As I begin to make our relationship my first priority, will you gently show me how? Thank you for loving me. Teach me how to best love you.

In Jesus' name,
Amen

DAY 3 Reflection

PUT DOWN THE MIRROR

"It's not about you."

Ever heard of *The Purpose Driven Life?* This is the first line of the book. Kind of a let down, right?

It was written by Rick Warren in 2002 and sat on the New York Time's Bestseller List for over 90 weeks. That's nearly 2 years! That's a lot of people seeking to find their purpose.

Ever heard of *What on Earth Am I Here For?* It's an updated version of *Purpose Driven Life* released to culminate the tenth anniversary of Warren's bestseller.

The first line in the new book?

"It's not about you."

Seems things haven't changed.

We have been enveloped with ads and quotes and books and commercials that keep our eyes on ourselves.

You need this phone so you can stay connected to the world.

You need this nutritional plan so you can stay focused on your health.

You need this car so you can impress your coworkers.

You need this line of credit so that you can purchase your dream boat.

You need...

"It's not about you."

Why would Warren open with such a statement? Does it make you want to keep reading further? To be told that maybe we're not all that important? That maybe our lives don't really matter?

Isn't there a small part of us that thinks, "Really?" If it's not about me, then why am I even here? What's my purpose? When is it going to be about me?

When someone hurts us, we ask, "What did I ever do to you?"

When a loved one passes away, we ask, "Why is this happening to me?"

When we lose our job, we ask, "What did I do wrong?"

When someone else gets that promotion, we ask, "When is it my turn?"

I. Me. My.

It was just before the Passover Festival.
Jesus knew that the hour had come for him
to leave this world and go to the Father. Having
loved his own who were in the world, he loved
them to the end.

The evening meal was in progress, and the devil had
already prompted Judas, the son of Simon Iscariot,
to betray Jesus. Jesus knew that the Father had put
all things under his power, and that he had come
from God and was returning to God; so he got up
from the meal.

John 13: 1–4a

This passage gets to me.

The scene here is that Jesus is at what we call "The Last Supper." Jesus knows that the hour was here for his death. The hour. He knows that the devil has already spurred Judas to betray Him. So, Jesus gets up from the meal...

I stopped the scripture here because I think we should pause and ask ourselves what *we* would be doing if we were in Jesus' place.

Would we get up and make an emotional speech about how we were about to die?

Wouldn't we want some sympathy or for people to know what a martyr we were about to be?

Wouldn't we want to stand up and point at Judas and let everyone know that he was about to betray us and so "ya'll make sure he gets what's coming to him!"

What does Jesus do here? Let's pick up where we left off.

So he got up from the meal, took off his outer cloth-
ing, and wrapped a towel around his waist. After
that, he poured water into a basin and began to
wash his disciples' feet, drying them with the towel
that was wrapped around him.

He came to Simon Peter, who said to him, "Lord,
are you going to wash my feet?"
Jesus replied, "You do not realize now what I am
doing, but later you will understand."

John 13:4–7

My goodness can you see it? Do you feel it?

I would be trembling too hard to tie anything around my waist and pour water into a basin and kneel down so calmly.

I would be nauseated with fear of what was coming.

I would be busting at the gut to tell everyone what was about to happen.

But if I did, all eyes would be on me. All compassion, sympathy and protectiveness would be centered on me. Feel sorry for me. Look at me.

For even the Son of Man did not come to be served,
but to serve, and to give his life as a ransom
for many.

Mark 10:45

It's not about me.

It's not about you.

Everything Jesus did while he walked the earth was at the direction of his Father. He knew his Father had a good plan, that it had a purpose that would make an eternal impact on lives until the end of our time here and he knew that we would be better served if he pointed us all to his Father rather than to his own life.

Everything. All of it.

Jesus didn't hold a mirror. He didn't keep glancing at his problems and his frustrations and the unfairness that kept coming his way. He didn't lean in to his own reflection (like I've done so many times) and question over and over again "why me?" or "what now?"

Jesus didn't gather his friends around and ask for their pity. He didn't manipulate others into constantly asking him if he was OK. He didn't. It wasn't about him.

It's not about us...the question is, do we understand that we still have purpose? That there's a reason we're all here and breathing? That we are a part of God's divine plan?

We have purpose. We are important. We are so loved by the Creator that He chose to demonstrate that to us through the sacrifice of His son. His beloved.

Let's follow Jesus' lead and serve others without the expectation of return service.

There was purpose in the life of Jesus.

There is purpose in the lives we lead.

Let's just put the mirror down.

Lord,

Thank you for loving me so sacrificially. For setting the ultimate example of service in the face of fear. Help me to serve others well. To see the needs that are right here in my corner of the world. Help me to tie a towel of service around my waist and humbly meet the needs of those who need you.

In Jesus' name,
Amen

Day 4 Reflection

HIS WAY IS LOVE

*Trust in the Lord and do good; dwell in the land
and enjoy safe pasture.
Take delight in the Lord, and he will give you the
desires of your heart.*

Psalm 37:3–4

That moment when you are so laser focused on this one important circumstance to change and suddenly you realize that while you were so focused in its direction, windows were opening behind you. Curtains were blowing. Sunshine was streaming in. Desires that have been held down deep are lulled to the surface, scratching their way up to breathe in the fresh air that is making its way into your world. That moment when you realize that the thing you were so focused on almost kept you from feeling the cool winds change right at your back.

Sometimes I find myself fixing my energies, prayers, attention, brain power and such, on something so fully that I am missing out on what is happening in my peripheral vision. I can recall this happening to me twice recently. I nearly missed it. I almost lost out on the vast, beautiful release that was happening right in my midst because I put my focus in the wrong direction for far too long.

This scripture is a promise. A plan to give me the desires of my heart. But I have to do my part.

- It starts by trusting that whatever the Lord has for me, is good.
- We've got to be where He put us...stay on His piece of land.
- Our relationship with Him must be priority.
- We need to be all in with Him, letting the Lord guide.

These things are an issue of the heart. And when our hearts line up with His, He will give us the desires of our heart. Why? Because when we are doing these things, His desires for us become our own. We begin to want what He wants for us. We begin to learn that His ways are in our best interest. That it is all about love. His love for us.

And just when it's not about us anymore, He opens that window and we suddenly realize that by seeking after His plan for us, He had something better in mind than we could have ever imagined.

When we chase Him down and trust, and dwell, and take delight, and commit and trust some more, we find that not only did we ultimately receive the desire of our hearts, but there is usually a ripple of blessings that come with that desire. And those ripples, those swelling waves, they take the blessing to a whole other level.

The tension eases in our entire world.

The priority that has been taking up so much space in our minds and hearts is suddenly evened out.

The goodness that is wrapping us from behind is distracting us from the thing that was driving us crazy just moments before.

What are you so in tune with that you may not recognize the other blessings around you? What has captivated your attention so strongly that you are stiff and rigid and fighting headaches because you need a release of pressure so badly? What is it?

When we keep our gaze on Him, there is joy and safety as we dwell, as we linger, in His presence.

Lord,

As I learn about you, I love you even more. Thank you for drawing me to a safe place where there is provision and contentment. Thank you for sharing your desires for this life and promising to give me those. What a gift. What great hope this gives me to look forward to.

In Jesus' name,
Amen

Day 5 Reflection

YOUR TIME IS NOW

Not long ago, I was in the nail salon. Oftentimes there is a language barrier between me and the nail technician and this time was no different. But she wanted to talk, and so talk we did.

As the flat-screen TV played in the background, news reports were being aired of another tragedy in our country involving innocent lives being taken in the name of evil. Just because.

This precious woman kept looking up to my face to talk to me. Oftentimes, she rolled her chair away to take a few seconds to accurately pronunciate what it is she wanted to say. I understood every word.

Her young son had just told her that morning that there was no hope for our country. He was asking her why he should go to school and continue to move forward with life when so much tragedy and fear was gripping those around him.

She assured him that he was safe, gave him a hug, and sent him out to catch his school bus.

She was heartbroken. What mother wants to hear their child tell them that there is no hope? What I discovered while speaking with her was that she was grasping for some hope herself.

Who knows but that you have come to your royal position for such a time as this?

Esther 4:14b

There is a story told in the Bible about a young woman named Esther. Through circumstances that only God himself could have crafted, she was placed in a position she never saw herself in. During this particular time of her life, she had the opportunity to voice her opinion to someone of power. An opinion that could cost her her life. She could have chosen to keep her mouth closed. To fade into the background. To leave it to someone else.

But her dear friend Mordecai urged her to speak. He proposed to her that perhaps she had been put into this hard place, at this time, "for such a time as this."

She boldly spoke. She risked her life for the sake of others.

Her obedience changed the course of history.

Have you ever felt like you were placed in a moment that had a bigger purpose than you had planned?

God has His eye on you. He knew from the beginning of time that you would be here, in this moment. He knew what your address would be today, the hurts and triumphs that brought you to this place and most importantly, the people that would be in your life ... even if for a brief moment in time ...to offer hope ... to offer truth.

> *Light in a messenger's eyes brings joy to the heart,*
> *and good news gives health to the bones.*

> *Proverbs 15:30*

I was getting a pedicure. Who knew that I would leave there feeling humbled that God would allow me to encourage this sweet lady. That I would have had the opportunity to point someone beyond what is happening in our brief lifetime to deposit words into her that would continue to work actively even if I never saw her again. To give a smile. A hug. And yes, a big tip.

God has brought us to this place. For this time. With these people. Let's guard against worrying what others might think of us. Let's keep our eye on the only One who really matters. What a privilege it is to know that the creator of all things wants to use you and me to bring hope and light to all people!

He is the only one who offers a hope that is everlasting and surpasses the momentary troubles of this world. So keep your eye out. You never know when or where an opportunity will arise. Where God will place you. Whose

encouragement. Whose soul is longing
... their creator.

...en you question your circumstances. When you're
not even paying attention. When things are going good,
and when things are going bad. Perhaps it's not about you...
it's not about *us*. It could be that we were placed in those
moments for a greater purpose "for such a time as this."

Lord,

*Thank you for giving me purpose in this life. A purpose
that spans beyond what my eyes see and my heart feels. Help
me to see every opportunity to love on others as a chance to
express my love for you.*

In Jesus' name,
Amen

FRAME It!

1. Does loving God seem intimidating to you? Why or why not?

2. Based on the definition of love found in 1 Corinthians 13:4–8, what comes easy for you? What is a challenge for you?

3. Oftentimes our love for others is born out of thankfulness for who they are and how they have impacted our lives. With that in mind, think of some examples in your own life when God expressed His own love for you.

4. Based on the reading this week, how can you demonstrate your love for God in a practical manner? Jot down one or two ideas here.

PART II

Love People

Loving Yourself

If we are to love our neighbors as we love ourselves, I think we need to first admit that sometimes we find it difficult to have self-love. Why would Jesus want us to love others as we love ourselves when we allow ourselves to be lead by our feelings and our circumstances on a regular basis?

We are too unpredictable. Christ knew not to hinge our relationships with others on how we feel about ourselves.

So how do we do it?

The answer is found in the most important command.

> *"Teacher, which is the greatest commandment in the Law?" Jesus replied: "Love the Lord your God with all your heart and with all your soul and with all your mind. This is the first and greatest commandment."*
>
> *Matthew 22:36–38*

We cannot love ourselves fully if we don't love Christ wholly.

It's only through loving Him, studying Him, spending time with Him, that we realize how much He loves us. The grace that He blankets us with on a daily basis, is found in His scriptures. The pages of His Word are saturated with the mercy that He has on His people, the forgiveness that He offers, the instruction that we are not the judge and He is, it's all in black and white when we love Him with all of our heart, soul and mind.

If we are not following His command of loving Him first and foremost, we will never understand how to love others the way that He tells us too.

What Holds Us Back?

Have you ever been invited to a bridal shower or to church or to coffee with a friend and you decided to just say *no*?

I have.

Why do we do that?

Our lives are busy. We have our own little family and our own little friend bubble and if we try to do something new, we might find that we've lost a couple of hours of scrolling through social media or binging on that Netflix series.

Maybe we say no because we are afraid of feeling lonely in a crowded room. It's a valid fear. You go with a friend to meet her friends and after a while, you don't know what to talk about or who to stand in the corner with while you drink your punch. Possibly, you've approached a group that you hear talking about the latest movie and when you offer your opinion, the crowd grows quiet. It doesn't mean that we've misspoken, but it can sure make us feel that way. Rejection comes in all forms.

Are you an introvert or an extrovert? If you have a natural tendency to stay to yourself, this would be a great place to hang all of the reasons why you can't engage with people you hardly know. The problem with labeling ourselves like this and refusing to engage because of it is that Christ wouldn't tell us to do something that He wouldn't equip us to do.

Maybe He did make some of us a little quieter, a little less social, but He intends to use it to bring us closer to Him and allow His love for us to pour out onto others. He may bring you through a transformation and pull you from your shell. He may use it to help you recognize when you are in the midst of others like you so that you can love them the way that He would love them.

Busyness, fear, pride ... these are just some of reasons why we hesitate to engage with new people. They can also be why we withhold love from those who are in our little bubble. We're touchy. We tend to think too much about this. We might get our feelings hurt.

This takes us back to the most important command again. When we love Christ with everything we've got, we won't allow our feelings to dictate our actions. We will be led by His Spirit. And there is no fear in the perfect love that He has for us.

There is no fear in love. But perfect
love drives out fear.

I John 4:18

Team Work

A few years ago, I found myself heavily burdened by the plight that a single mom has on a daily basis. I don't know how to explain where it came from except I believe God himself was giving me a small peak into their lives. I've known single moms in my lifetime. Some of them are no longer single and some of them remain that way. I never felt that they confided any great hidden mystery about their lives in me, but I am an observer. I pay attention to what they say and how they live their lives.

One particular Christmas season, the Lord opened my spiritual eyes up to a quick picture of what I believe how the majority of single moms feel in the church setting. I envisioned women sitting on church pews, physically tired from being both mom and dad all week long, and wondering if the church even knew that they existed and that their needs are a little different from what the typical family requires. I envisioned women who work hard at their jobs all week long and then return to their home at the end of the day, feeling tired, frustrated over their lack of financial resources, and guilt ridden that their children aren't experiencing a home that has a mommy and a daddy.

I wept that day as I saw the faces of women who love God and want to bring up their children in the teachings of Jesus but on the inside were struggling to see where they fit in their local church. Most churches don't cater to single parents. If you want to go to a traditional Sunday school class, you have to choose between the young married class, older couples' class, or women's class (which usually brings in women whose husbands are teaching somewhere else in the church during that time). That's not to say that all churches operate this way, but from my experience, it can place single moms in a position of not knowing where they fit in.

As time marched on from that day, I began asking God why I felt such a burden and how was I to give God glory through that. I began studying the scriptures to see what God had to say about single mothers. I took notes on practical ways that believers could be helping single moms. I researched what some churches were doing to support and encourage their single parents.

As I became more and more passionate about wanting to do something, I began asking God to show me who could come alongside me to do some work. In a matter of a few days, I called on an older, wiser woman in my life and shared with her what God was doing to my heart. It *just so happens* that in the previous weeks, another woman in our church had approached this same older, wiser woman and expressed to her that she'd like to work with single moms. She asked our mutual friend to help her pray about how she could begin taking action on behalf of the single moms in our own church. I was absolutely thrilled! Not only had God provided someone so quickly to lock arms with me on this cause, but it was confirmed to me on the phone that day that I wasn't just making this stuff up in my own head. God was really at work, talking to me, and preparing me for what was ahead.

That's how He works. He knows the big picture and He is always working in our lives preparing us and equipping us to do what He has called us to do for His kingdom. What I want you to grasp here is that once we are a child of God, we have spiritual brothers and sisters that He intends for us to come alongside and get to know so that we can work together to bring Him glory. The woman that I partnered with, who felt passionate about the same issue I did, became a very good friend of mine.

When we resist this command to love others as we love ourselves, we miss out on so much.

Through this season in my life, I gained so much more than I gave. It wasn't because of anything I did, it was because I was obedient. I stepped out from my comfort zone and chased after something that is near and dear to our Father's heart. Orphans and widows.

Religion that God our Father accepts as pure and faultless is this: to look after orphans and widows in their distress.

James 1:27

I gained a new ministry friend. My reliance on Christ grew exponentially and He did nothing but prove Himself over and over again. Single mothers in our church, as well as the friends that they invited into this ministry, were encouraged. Some of their needs were met through our meetings. Spiritual and tangible needs. Children in these homes were coming home from school to mothers who were growing in their faith. To mothers who knew they had a solid support system in place. Someone to go to court with them. Someone to help provide Christmas for the children. Friendship. Prayer partners.

> *I've been given friends who've been through challenging struggles and we've become prayer partners. I know I can count on their prayers no matter what—such a bond! So thankful!*

> *Lynda*

These are just a few of the benefits that we saw as we loved these ladies in the same way we would like to be loved. It's been many years since this season has passed and I believe the ripple effect of our obedience is continuing today. Perhaps one day we'll see where it all spread too.

Fear

Loving others as Christ asks us to do isn't just about engaging with people outside of our sphere, it's about how we love those who we are doing life with on a day-to-day basis.

Our spouses, our children, our co workers, our siblings, and parents ... I've experienced for myself that sometimes the people closest to us are the ones that can hurt us the easiest. That flips the other direction as well. These people are the ones that *we* have the most opportunity to hurt and take for granted too.

It's sometimes easier to lavish love on total strangers than it is to love on someone we do life with day in and day out.

While we can let fear hold us back from loving strangers, it can also restrain us when it comes to loving friends and family as Christ loves us.

It makes sense. We already have a history with these people. We know their strengths and weaknesses. We've been affected by the sin in their life. They've seen us at our best and our worst.

It's hard to forgive as Christ forgives when we know we might continue to be hurt by someone's actions. It's hard to be merciful when we see no attempt on someone else's part to change for the better. It's hard to comfort someone who has never comforted us when we needed it for ourselves.

The root of what holds us back here is usually tied to fear.

The same things that we fear when it comes to approaching strangers can also be the things we fear when it comes to our every-day life circle of friends and family.

If I suddenly begin to show love to my co workers in a way they've never seen before, they may not accept it. And if they don't accept my new way of loving, they may reject *me*.

If I suddenly begin to engage more with my aging parents, investing my time and attention like they've never seen before, I could become too busy. What if I drop the ball on this? Will they be forgiving? Will they understand?

If I begin to forgive every single time my spouse hurts me or my child disobeys, will my heart be crushed from here on out? Will it only cause me to become resentful and bitter and not do a lick of good for my family?

Fear is only a four-letter word but boy, does it pack a punch.

False Evidence Appearing Real.

I've heard this acronym used since I was a child. It's a pretty accurate definition of fear. God's word tells us to fear not. In fact, that statement is made several hundred times through the New and Old Testaments.

Fear is a problem that we live with day in and day out. It's a head issue. As women, we can be great at playing out all the possible scenarios when we are making a life change. We can come up with too many endings to count and by the time we are finished thinking them all through, we've lost our courage to follow through with the first step of obedience.

Never Give Up

My son came out of the womb strong-willed. We came home from the hospital twenty-four hours after his birth and I don't think he slept more than three hours over the next three days. He dictated our schedule, hard, in the beginning.

As he began to grow into a busy, chatty, all-boy boy, we found ourselves becoming exhausted. We seemed to be more exhausted than most parents we knew. It took us a while to figure it out, but our son was in fact strong-willed to the core. We seriously weren't prepared for this as young twenty-something parents.

Although he exhausted us, he was pure joy. He burned so much energy during the days that as he got older, he began to require close to twelve hours of sleep each night. Those nights were heaven!

As time drove on and he became a teenager who was taller than me and more quick witted than anyone we knew, disciplining him became hard to do. It seemed that any guardrail we put up in his life, he was going to slide his hand across to look for weak spots. He was inquisitive. A quick learner. And his desire for independence and adventure seemed to lead his actions more so than his desire to honor his parents.

Fast forward to his high school years.

Our beautiful, strong-willed, joyful son had trouble in school. One year his principal told us "he just has so much personality, he doesn't know where to put it all." Boy, was that an understatement! He was like fitting a square peg into a round hole in a conventional classroom. His teachers loved him as they saw how undeniably smart he was, and that he had leadership ability, but he just wasn't mature enough yet to know what all of that meant.

As a teenager, he would threaten to move out and live with friends that were no good for him. My husband would say, "Just let him go, I'm so sick of this!" Those were his emotions talking. We would dig into scripture and see that even though our son was becoming more independent, he was still our responsibility. More than that, he did not realize the effect his actions would have on him later in life. It was our job to keep those guardrails up even if it meant leaning in with every bit of our body weight and pulling all-nighters.

At times, we were fearful of what our lives would look like as we continued hold up those guardrails for another two years. Again, we dug into scripture, looked at how Christ loves us even when we are trying to pull away from Him, and we would dig back in. The ripple effect of quitting high school was too great for his future; he just didn't know it yet.

Despite our fear of driving ourselves into sickness because of the exhaustion, despite our fear of what other families were thinking of our son's actions, despite our fears that we could invest all of this energy and time cheering him into adulthood all to have him throw his upbringing into the trash can as he left (it's always a possibility, isn't it?), we kept our face in the scriptures. We frequently quoted Matthew 22:37–40 to one another as a reminder.

> *Jesus replied: "Love the Lord your God with all your heart and with all your soul and with all your mind." This is the first and greatest commandment. And the second is like it: "Love your neighbor as yourself." All the Law and the Prophets hang on these two commandments.*

> *Matthew 22:37–40*

Our son was our neighbor.

As we pressed on, we did our best to love him as we would want to be loved. If I had threatened to move in with people who weren't good for me, I would hope that someone would try to stop me. If I was threatening to quit high school, I would hope that someone would see the big picture when I couldn't and cheer me on to stay put.

Christ doesn't give up on us and this is how we love our neighbor as ourselves.

Never fear. Never give up. Always hope.

Lord,

You know that I've been hurt in the past when I've tried to love others. You know the fears that I have when it comes to this. Help me stay close to you. Keep me reminded that love never fails and I can never go wrong extending love to others. Continue to teach me your example and guide me in your way.

In Jesus' name,
Amen

DAY 1 Reflection

BE EASY ON YOURSELF

I was recently talking with a friend and she said something that resonated deeply with me.

We were talking about goals and dreams and what may be out in front of us that we want to attain. We were talking about how to get to those places and how sometimes we have to muddle through other things, let other things go, clear a path, and so on before we can reach those goals. It was a wonderful conversation soaked with truth.

I thought we were going to keep talking about big, personal goals and encourage each other to keep pursuing them. I thought we were going to go big picture. I was wrong.

She said something that rang a bell deep in my heart.

I'm learning to give myself grace in the everyday things. To celebrate those accomplishments, even if they're small.

Isn't that good?

Don't we wait until the *big* thing is checked off our list before we cut ourselves a break and celebrate? Before we acknowledge that we've accomplished anything at all? Aren't women known for being their own worst critics? For being so focused on the big, giant goals that we push aside the small steps that had to be accomplished before reaching that destination?

Here's what I'm learning the older I get and the more that I make relationships with other women a priority...we are too hard on ourselves. Way too hard.

> *But he said to me, "My grace is sufficient for*
> *you, for my power is made perfect in weakness."*
> *Therefore, I will boast all the more gladly about my*
> *weaknesses, so that Christ's power may rest on me.*
> *That is why, for Christ's sake, I delight in weak-*
> *nesses, in insults, in hardships, in persecutions,*
> *in difficulties. For when I am weak,*
> *then I am strong.*
>
> *2 Corinthians 12:9–10*

If you struggle to simply get out of bed some mornings because of anxiety or depression, and you actually get up ... cut yourself a break. Acknowledge that you just accomplished something. It doesn't matter if it is a "hard" thing to anyone else. If it is "hard" for you, and you pushed through ... give yourself some grace.

If you are fighting with your spouse five or six times a day and you have a day where you only fuss four ... don't linger over the four, celebrate the absence of the others. It's a small thing that can lead to bigger things.

Mothers of young children, I hear many of you voice your desire to have your quiet time in the morning and get in your work-out, shower and start breakfast all before that baby wakes up. Some of you are drowning with guilt because you haven't had your child's thirty-day pictures taken like everyone else has (bahahaha..ask me how many times I had my children's pictures taken when they were babies) and now your child will grow up with low self-esteem because you didn't document every inch that they grew! Stop! There are more of you than you think only getting a shower every other day and barely managing to feed your husband after coming in from a long day of work a bowl of cereal.

If you're that mom and you got out of bed and loved on your children today, celebrate that you took care of what was most important. If at the end of the day only one thing out of eight things is ticked off your to-do list, celebrate the one thing and start fresh tomorrow.

It's important to set goals. To reach for the stars and move forward with vision and purpose. But while you move forward, give yourselves some grace and acknowledge that *even the small accomplishments are still accomplishments*. It takes plowing through the small things before the big things can be attained.

God is in the details and it's in those achievements that sometimes our intimacy with Him is more tangible than others. It's those small tasks that when achieved, draw out a quiet *"yesssssss"* and will draw our gaze to our Father, who is so pleased and just tickled when we include Him in those mini celebrations.

He sees when we struggle to get out of bed, but we do it anyway. He sees when we are unhappy with our jobs, but we go and give it our best anyway. He sees when our anxiety tells us to stay home, but we push through and call that friend anyway. He sees when we push away the cake in an attempt to care for our bodies. He sees when that baby has kept you up all night and it's all that you can do the next day to simply brush your teeth.

"My power is made perfect in weakness."

In our weak moments, let's let Him in and share that. We have a tendency to beat ourselves up and assume that God is disappointed when we struggle. That He is somehow never satisfied with our small steps. Not so. *It is in our weakness that He has room to work*. It is here that He shines through. It's this place that we realize our need for His power and comfort and He delivers—every single time.

Let's lean in. Be more like my friend and celebrate the small things. Celebrate *with* Him. He's right there lending His power to help us push through. Then, let's throw a little praise party as we accept the grace that He is handing us!

Lord,

Thank you for loving us not just through the big things, but through the small things. Learning to love people the way that you do will only need slight changes to my mindset and lifestyle but at times, they can seem monumental. Help me keep a proper perspective. You wouldn't task me with something that couldn't be done.

In Jesus' name,
Amen

DAY 2 Reflection

WE ARE BUILT FOR FRIENDSHIP

If you don't consider yourself a "runner," have you ever tried it? Have you ever laced up your tennis shoes, thrown on a hat and taken off down the street for a jog? You probably figured out real quick that it's not as easy as it looks, especially when you're alone.

After just a few minutes the body starts to warm up, the calves start to stiffen, the shins start to burn and the lungs just can't keep up. That's when you slow back to a walk and start asking yourself "What on earth was I thinking?"

On the flip side of that, have you ever gone out as a new runner and taken a friend or two with you? You meet up at the local track, do some stretches in the parking lot, and start with smiles and a warm-up walk. After a few minutes of that, you're ready to jog. You can hear your friends breathing *just as loud as you* (*yes*, Jesus!) and you identify with their struggle. You may be ready to slow down but there's just something about running with friends that helps keep you going further. By the end of your time together, you're high-fiving and proud of your accomplishment, even if it takes a few minutes to catch your breath.

There's something about doing it together that makes it a little easier.

When I am walking through something hard, my closest friends are a source of encouragement. They send me texts with just a few words to push me forward and keep a smile on my face. They let me know when they've prayed for me and they make sure I'm not isolating myself, and I try to do the same for them.

The flip side is we have fun together! Human contact is priceless. We solve a lot of problems when we go antiquing or grab a meal together. We go back home to our families feeling refreshed and ready to tackle whatever comes next.

Friendship. Camaraderie. Belonging. People who "get you."

This is a gift that is meant for you. A rich, fluid gift that God uses at times to take care of our needs, to bring us joy and to encourage and lift us up.

God's word says this:

> *And let us consider how we may spur one another
> on toward love and good deeds.*

Hebrews 10:24

We were created for relationship. That whole "hands and feet of Jesus" thing, this is our playground for it.

Jesus himself did life with friends. He had twelve who walked with him throughout his ministry. He held three of those closer than the rest. He had one betray him in the end.

Can you relate?

A large circle, a smaller circle within those and one who loses their way.

I relate. Jesus gets this, He's been there, and I can talk to him about all of it.

I have been reminded this season just how unpredictable our lives can be. That they can be cut short in an instant. These relationships, this is where the good stuff is. This is where our souls can find satisfaction and the thirst we have for deep conversation and authenticity can be quenched.

Can I encourage you to step out? To send that text or speak to that mom in the carpool line even if with fear and trembling? We need each other. We were *built* to need each other. But sometimes you and I must take the first step in starting a new friendship.

By yourself you're unprotected.
With a friend you can face the worst.
Can you round-up a third?
A three-stranded rope isn't easily snapped.

Ecclesiastes 4:12 (The Message)

The enemy would have you isolate yourself. He'll use your weaknesses and try to convince you that you should keep your distance. The enemy will also keep you too busy with *good* things to make the time to spend with others. He has a big bag of tricks and he's not afraid to use them.

A friendship that reflects Biblical principles is a dangerous thing in the eyes of your enemy. You may think that he could not care less...that's another lie.

Be on guard. You may have to fight to keep some people in your life and they may fight for you to be in theirs if you're putting up walls.

If I could sit down with you over a coffee and implore you to make the effort to engage and seek out these relationships, I would have my purse in hand already.

Put friendship on your priority list. Ask the Lord to send those that you need, and to push away the ones that are meant for someone else.

You need this.

They need *you.*

We are better together.

Lord,

Something about this seems scary. In order to have friends and be a friend, I must be authentic. I must remove layers of myself. I have to be vulnerable. Thank you, as anything in your plan is ultimately for my own good. I trust you. Open my eyes to those with whom I need to spend time with and to those I need to let go.

In Jesus' name,
Amen

Day 3 Reflection

BUILD A FIRE AND THEY WILL COME

In the same way, let your light shine before others,
that they may see your good deeds and glorify your
Father in heaven.

Matthew 5:16

I've read this scripture many times over the years. It's pretty popular. In my mind, I always pictured someone ... me ... holding a flashlight. Then my brain would envision those guys at airports who use light in their hands to guide the enormous planes to safety. Small yet powerful beams of light pointing the way.

That's not my picture anymore.

Now I see fire!

Fire has the power to do things that flashlights just can't. If my good deeds have the power to point people to Christ, I'd say that's pretty powerful.

Fire brings warmth: we can be inviting and welcoming.
Fire is full of colors ... our good deeds won't all look the same, different passions—diverse interests—endless possibilities.
Fire can be used to direct ... good deeds can point people in the right direction, lingering effects of our actions can ripple out into eternity.
Fire has an unmistakable sound ... our actions and voice are unique to who we are, no one else has our gifts, our interests, or our stories.
Fire draws out what has been in the darkness ... we can peek at others' curiosity, get people moving.
Fire melts away dross ... our good deeds can help others peel away the layers that have them bound up and stuck.

Let's be warm and inviting. Let's actively share God's goodness with others. Make a little noise. Cause others to take note and be curious. Give direction to those who have stumbled off the path that has been set out for them.

I love how The Message translation of the Bible speaks Matthew 5 verses 14–16:

> *Here's another way to put it: You're here to be light, bringing out the God-colors in the world. God is*

not a secret to be kept. We're going public with this, as public as a city on a hill. If I make you light-bearers, you don't think I'm going to hide you under a bucket, do you? I'm putting you on a light stand. Now that I've put you there on a hilltop, on a light stand—shine! Keep open house; be generous with your lives. By opening up to others, you'll prompt people to open up with God, this generous Father in heaven.

You are here to bring out the God *colors* in the world. To be generous. To open up to others.

Your actions have the power to prompt people to open up to God. Your good deeds can be used to cause others to glorify God. He wants to use your life to point others to him.

Do good deeds. Do them.

He has put you on a light stand. Given you a place to stretch, flicker, crackle, and shine. Not for ourselves, but for Him.

How will others know how we have peace in times of loss if we don't build a fire and invite them to come and hear our stories? How will they know what kept us going while raising strong-willed teenagers ... or what's the secret to a long, happy marriage?

I have found that people are hungry to hear our stories. Not just the good stuff we post on social media, but the real-life challenges and triumphs we all share. For those of us who have placed our hope and faith in God, we must lay ourselves open. We are called to brag openly about him through word and deed.

Let's throw some wood on our fires. Stoke the ashes. Create some sparks.

Let's open our homes. Give to those in need. Be proactive. Make a difference. In so doing, others will be more open to God. We will cause others to look to him. We will cause others to look *for* him. And friends, *we* will be blessed.

Lord,

How exciting that you want me to be a bright light to those around me! Thank you for this privilege. I don't take it lightly. (See what I did there? God has a sense of humor too.) I pray as others are drawn to me, that you will shine through me, bringing others warmth, direction, and hope.

In Jesus' name,
Amen

Day 4 Reflection

WHEN SITTING SHOULDER TO SHOULDER IS ALL YOU CAN DO

What do we say to someone who has suffered great loss?

How can we adequately express the deep sorrow we feel for someone when they are in mourning?

I recently had the privilege of hearing someone speak at a memorial service and they said something like this:

> *What if we all acted like sponges? When those around us are hurting, we sit close and absorb some of their burdens for them.*

That may not sound like a very welcoming invitation, but it has stuck with me.

God's word says to "rejoice with those who rejoice and mourn with those who mourn."

Merriam-Webster says this:

Definition of *mourn*
<u>intransitive verb</u>
1. to feel or express grief or sorrow

I love that mourning is a verb. A feeling that can be expressed and the expression doesn't have to be with words. We don't even have to speak.

We can grieve over many things:

- A marriage that is ending
- A healthy body that has now been diagnosed with an illness
- The loss of a dream
- Failure of a business
- Death of a loved one
- A wayward child
- A close friendship that is ending
- A broken heart

Here's where the sponge comes in.

When a loved one is hurting and we lean in and allow ourselves to feel what they feel, we become spongy... absorbent.

When someone is shedding tears, we can slide right over and absorb some of that sorrow with them. And when they are rejoicing, we get to soak up some of the exhilaration they are feeling too.

What happens when a sponge takes on water? It comes to life!

When we allow God to use us, He brings life into our bones. Like a sponge that puffs out and becomes soft and pleasant to hold on to, we too become a soft place for others to lean in to and we are smack in the middle of where God is working.

This is one way that we help to carry one another's burdens.

When we become spongy:

1. We help soak up some of the sadness in the lives of others and remove it so that they aren't wading in it from the ankles to their waist.
2. Like a sponge, we come to life. As a dry, porous material crashes into wet tears of sorrow, we expand. Our capacity to take on and take in grief and sadness grows as we become agents of God's sustaining grace.

Many times, when someone near us is going through something hard, it's easy to become a little gun shy and to back up and let someone else comfort them. What would I say? How can I help?

Just show up.

It's okay to not have the right words or not have any words at all. Slide alongside that friend and wrap your arm around them. Cry and snot and shake with them. Hold their hand. Serve them a glass of cold water. Fold their laundry. These are all actions and they do not require words.

God's word says,

> *God blesses those people who grieve. They will find*
> *comfort!*

Matthew 5:4

Perhaps God wants to use you to help bring comfort to someone.

Your presence is enough. It is a gift to those who need help absorbing all that has them wrecked. We don't ask people if they would like to receive a gift, we simply give it.

Don't let your nerves keep you from moving on this. If God has put someone on your heart who is grieving something, go to them. Just show up.

Those are sacred tears they are shedding and you will have the privilege of soaking up some of that grief. It will bring you to life. It will bring nourishment to your bones and you will be glad you moved.

May we all strive to be more porous. More pliable. Absorbers.

Agents of grace.

Lord,

As I continue to learn how to love others well, help me see
those around me through your eyes. Show me who needs

comforting. And give me the courage to step out and lean into them. Thank you for this privilege.

In Jesus' name,
Amen

Day 5 Reflection

THAT TIME GOD ASKED ME TO BE CARRIED

Some men came carrying a paralyzed man on a mat and tried to take him into the house to lay him before Jesus. When they could not find a way to do this because of the crowd, they went up on the roof and lowered him on his mat through the tiles into the middle of the crowd, right in front of Jesus.

Luke 5:18–19

A few years ago, my husband took a bad fall at work. He fell off a roof while working alone, landing on his head, knocking him out cold. When he came to, he had no idea where he was, but he did manage to call me in his drunken stupor. That was one of the scariest days of my life.

After racing to be by his side, with our two small children at my hip, we watched him be transported to the local hospital. I drove as quick as I could and arrived at the E.R. just moments after my guy. To my surprise, I was greeted by a handful of men from our church. In all the frenzy of getting Tim help, our church was alerted to begin praying and all the staff jumped in a car to meet us as we arrived. Wow.

By the end of that day, we were all back home. My man had a lump on his head the size of a baseball, but no permanent damage was found. We contemplated that if he had fallen just a little to the right or left, he could have easily been stabbed by the tools in his belt, or something worse.

We were blessed.

My husband and I are servants. We make dinners. He uses his skills to bless widows. Our home is always open to those needing some rest. We especially enjoy taking care of things and people when no one is watching. When no one is aware. We are perfectly content to find out later how an anonymous blessing affected someone rather than tie our name to it.

That's our wheelhouse.

But that day, God asked me to *take* help instead of *giving* it.

Can I tell you, it was a little *uncomfortable*?

He asked me to stop worrying that I may be putting someone out so that they could help our family in our time of need. He asked me to relax, to be thankful and to let the people in our lives take care of us for a day or two.

He asked me to let our friends and family carry our mat.

The details of that day were taken care of without an utterance of concern from my lips.

My husband's truck was retrieved and deposited back into our driveway. I still don't know who did that. My children were taken care of by someone else while we waited for test results. I honestly can't remember who had them. Our dinner that night was taken care of before we even arrived back home.

Looking back, it was as if we were literally being carried on all four corners. We were given the freedom to focus on what was most important that day. My husband's well-being.

I'll never forget how loved we felt.

Most women I know are mat *carriers*. They jump in and do the work. They bring the meals. Watch the children. Organize the help. Prostrate in prayer. Fill the gap.

Have you ever been asked to lay down? Have you ever been put on a mat involuntarily?

You keep trying to get back up, but the Lord has someone place their hand on your proverbial forehead and tell you to lie still?

Sometimes it's necessary.

Not only for you and me to lie still, but there is a blessing in store for those carrying your mat.

We have to be careful not to steal that from others.

There is a time to serve and a time to be served.

Let's try to do a better job at recognizing where the Lord would have us. If He says to pick up someone else's mat, let's pick it up. If He says to lie down, let's lie down.

Lord,

I'll admit that I'm not the best at taking help from others. But, it's part of your plan and it's for my good, so I want to do better at this. When someone is trying to be a blessing to me or my family, help me to see your hand in it and accept it with humility and thanksgiving. Thank you for the privilege of being blessed by others.

In Jesus' name,
Amen

FRAME It!

1. How can it be hard to love others if we are having trouble loving ourselves?

2. Fear can talk us out of loving others, but courage can give us the push we often need. What are some benefits of quality relationships you have either experienced yourself or seen second hand?

3. Sometimes, the best way to love other people is to simply pray for them. How might praying for others help us to love them more?

4. Why do you think Christ values us loving others so greatly?

PART IV

Simple Faith

I get it, you're scared. Living all in for Jesus changes everything. And we don't like change, do we?

This will be a little uncomfortable. It may feel prickly or it may feel like a warm, inviting sweater on a cold, snowy day. I hope it's the latter. I hope that you're like how I've been in the past. Sick and tired of practicing religion that makes you feel restless. I hope you're ready to snuggle up to your Heavenly Father who is inviting you to something more restful.

A deeper relationship with Him and more meaningful relationships with others.

Our striving to live for Jesus keeps Jesus from living through us. When we are merely checking down a list of Christian "have tos," we are keeping Him at arm's length. I picture Jesus waiting patiently for us to realize there is a better way. *The* way.

Have you ever felt close to Jesus in the past? Perhaps you were in the habit at one time of spending quality time in His Word and in prayer. You disciplined yourself to spend time on your relationship but what kept you coming back was God Himself. You were hungry to know Him more and so you made that relationship top priority.

I was so hungry for a deeper understanding of Jesus in my twenties. It was a great time of learning and growing in my faith. I was involved in an in-depth Bible study that required about thirty minutes of my day reading and studying scripture. I started my time in prayer as I knew I couldn't learn a thing on my own.

One year, when my children were small and our study was on a summer break, I remember getting out of the habit of spending that daily, quality time with Jesus. It seemed that I was too tired to rise early or simply unfocused without a structured study to guide my reading. I got busy. I got distracted.

I missed out.

As summer drew to a close, and Bible study started again, I realized that I had missed out on getting to know Jesus without the disciplines from the study. I got a picture in my mind that fall season that I'll never forget.

Each morning as I had gotten up early to spend time in the Word, not only did I look forward to it, but Jesus did too. I'm his daughter. What father doesn't love spending one-on-one time with their child? Our days together went from nearly an hour of uninterrupted time together, to thirty minutes, to fifteen, until finally, He *might* get the left-overs from my day in the evening. I pictured that Jesus was waiting for me each morning in our own little room. A table for two. He sat with His legs casually crossed, one hand in His lap and the other on a mug of hot coffee. As that summer marched on, I blew in and out of that room, too rushed to even take a seat after a while. Eventually, there were days that I walked right past the doorway, and I believe He was sitting, waiting.

Like I said, I missed out.

Don't do that.

We are not promised tomorrow, and I'll never forget how sad I was when I realized that I had blown months of time where I could have had the undivided attention of Jesus.

Stay Connected

We have loropetalum bushes in our back yard. They encircle half of our swimming pool and they are beautiful! The trunks are sturdy and thick near the ground, but the branches sprout out every which way. I don't care for manicured, perfectly round or square shrubs. These branches blow easy in a breeze and are low enough to provide shelter for families of rabbits that come and go here.

The thing is, they grow so fast that my husband winds up trimming them down at least twice during the summer months. They can grow several feet in a short amount of time if the weather is just right. At the beginning of this summer season, he decided to do something drastic. He cut them to within eighteen inches of the ground. He scalped them! Once all of the branches were cut away, he piled them in the wheel-barrow and pushed them off into the woods. Those delicate purple leaves will wilt and discolor lying on the ground. But after a few summertime showers, there is already new growth on those stumpy bushes now.

If I took those branches that were cut away from their trunk and planted them in fresh soil, would they grow on their own? No! They will not produce anymore leaves now that they've been pruned.

In John 15, Jesus tells us that He is the true vine and his Father is the gardener. Unless we are connected to Jesus, we will not produce spiritual fruit.

> *I am the vine; you are the branches. If you remain in me and I in you, you will bear much fruit; apart from me you can do nothing. If you do not remain in me, you are like a branch that is thrown away and withers; such branches are picked up, thrown into the fire and burned.*

John 15: 5–6

It's Not Always Springtime

When a branch is connected to its true vine, it has all that it needs to live the life it's been called to live. It has nourishment. It has support. It doesn't have to worry about what is crawling around on the ground because it is held just above the dirt.

Like healthy branches, we have everything we need for this life. That doesn't mean we won't have challenges. Even the most beautiful flowers have to weather storms. They weather droughts. They're even subjected to harsh sprays and chemicals to keep them from becoming infested with disease or bugs.

Sometimes, we need to remember this.

Loving God with all of our heart, soul and mind doesn't mean that we won't weather storms. Loving our neighbor as ourselves doesn't mean that at times, we won't feel like we've been sprayed with pepper spray, even when we are doing everything right. Even when we're growing healthy and staying connected to the true vine, we will still experience pain and suffering.

But hang on, the good stuff doesn't come from the outside, it comes from the deep. It comes from knowing that you are not just attached to the vine, but you are *in* the vine. Inside. Safe. Secure.

John 15 goes on to say this:

> *As the Father has loved me, so have I loved you. Now remain in my love ... I have told you this so that my joy may be in you and that your joy may be complete. My command is this: Love each other as I have loved you ... You did not choose me, but I chose you and appointed you so that you might go and bear fruit—fruit that will last—and so that whatever you ask in my name the Father will give you. This is my command: Love each other.*

> *John 15 :9–17*

If He tells us to remain in His love, it sounds like we have a choice. It's up to us. If we do this, we will bear much fruit.

What will that look like? It's different for everyone, but it's beautiful!

The fruit that we will bear, He says, will last. Meaning, it will out live us. It's fruit that will not perish or spoil and it will become a part of our legacy. Our testimony.

Good Fruit Never Dies

I said yes to a blind date one late Saturday night and met my husband then. When we became engaged, we started attending church together. I had gotten out of the habit at that time and frankly was ready to return to my Christian faith.

Before we knew it, most of our social time was spent at church softball games, chaperoning middle school student lock-ins, and attending small group socials with couples around our same age. Tim had grown up in this church and most of the guys we spent time with were lifelong friends for him.

It was a sweet time. Bridal showers, weddings, new home purchases, real, grown-up jobs. We were adulting and it felt great!

One particular evening we were invited to dinner with two of our best friends at their home. We ate, played cards, and had an absolute blast together. As evening wound down and we were walking out to our car, our friend Jeff yelled "We love ya'll! Marriage is fun! Just keep praying together."

Never in a million years did I ever think someone in their early twenties would give us that kind of advice.

Never. What I remember most about that was his boldness in what he said. I was so young in my faith. I would've been too embarrassed to give that advice. Wow. Not something I'm proud of now. But I learned that night that being bold is sometimes necessary. And authentic friendship holds nothing back. I also walked away knowing that he was loving us the way he would love himself. I don't know if anyone gave him and his new bride that advice, but I do know that he had a key to a healthy marriage and he wasn't going to keep it to himself.

Neither will I.

Loving Our Neighbors

In the book of Luke, Jesus tells a story about loving our neighbors. An expert in the law asks him the question, "What must I do to inherit eternal life?"

Jesus answers with a question, as He does frequently. "What is written in the law, how do you read it?"

The expert replied, "Love the Lord your God with all your heart and with all your soul and with all your strength and with all your mind' and 'Love your neighbor as yourself."

Ding, ding, ding! It seems that the two most important commands are really the real deal. They keep coming up!

The expert goes on to ask Jesus who his neighbor would be. Jesus tells a rather famous story about a man who is walking down the road and is attacked and robbed. He is left for dead, right out in the open. Two men walk right by him, choosing to pass on the other side of the road, ignoring that this man is in need. A third man happens upon the scene and goes into immediate action.

He treats the man's wounds, binding them up so that he can travel, loads the victim up on his donkey and takes him into town. There, he checks into a hotel room to care for the man and give him a place to rest and recover. He pays the bill to the hotel attendant, leaving the man to finish healing alone but with a promise to return and finish paying for any other expenses the injured man may incur.

He treats this man the way he would want to be treated. He takes care of him, shows him mercy. All without any hope or thought of receiving anything in return for his kindness. It's just what he does.

Our friend who hollered from his front door, urging us to begin praying as a couple, he was loving us like he would love himself. He was transferring information that was either given to him earlier in his marriage, or, this is information he would've liked for someone to give him.

He gave us a gift. A gift that if received and cared for, would live on beyond my life and our marriage. We would pass this on to others over the course of time. To our children, yes, but also to any other young couples who would cross our paths. As they accept this gift, this information, and put it into practice, tasting the sweet fruit that was bore through praying together, they too would pass on this advice.

Christ longs to see His children love one another, just as any father longs to see their children do the same. Not to merely co exist, but to live life together. To exchange advice. To suffer and mourn together and comfort one another. We are the hands and feet of Jesus and he intends to use all of us to bring that physical touch of comfort and audible voice of reason when we need it.

If we claim to love God with all our heart, soul, and mind, yet do not love our neighbor as ourselves, we aren't loving Him the way He has asked.

In showing love to others, we are expressing our love for Christ.

The two go together. And this is the church.

Anyone who believes in Christ as their savior and Lord is a sister or brother to anyone else who has entered in His family. He calls us the church. He is the head, and we make up the body. These buildings that sit on nearly every corner down here in the south are meeting places for God's family. A place to come together and make much of Him and leave making much of others in His name.

Christ calls us to a simple faith. We grow deeper in knowledge and wisdom as we spend time in His word and with other believers, yes. But it all still comes down to loving God and loving others.

Take inventory of your life. Write down what you do with your time. What are your responsibilities? What do you enjoy doing and what seems to cause you stress?

Now, pray over these for the next few days and weeks, asking God what you need to let go of and what you need to dive head-first into. Pour your current priorities through the sieve of the two most important commands in the Bible.

Sit on it for a while, then pour again if you need to.

God will honor your earnest prayer. It's time to lay down religion that makes us tired and weary. Man-made rules. Expectations that we put on ourselves or allow others to place on us.

It's time to embrace Christ with both arms. To curl up in his lap for some rest. To call him Abba Father with child-like faith and seek His direction and discernment.

He wants you right there. He won't let you down.

Lord,

Thank you for loving me. Thank you for this time to reset my priorities and line them up with yours. I'm a little tired. Change is usually uncomfortable. Help me to know when my discomfort is my own doing and when it is a gentle nudge from you. I want to love you and love others. Lead me to the people that can minister to me and lead me to those who need to be ministered to by me. I trust you, Lord.

In Jesus' name,
Amen

DAY 1 Reflection

ALL IN

*So they pulled their boats up on shore, left
everything and followed him.*

Luke 5:11

"Come on now, jump! One...two...three!"

As our son stood on the edge of the swimming pool,
I did my best to coax him to jump in. He stood, watching the other children do what their swim teachers were
instructing them to do.

They were laying on mini boards, kicking their legs.
Some were practicing blowing bubbles in the water. They
were laughing and splashing. He wanted so bad to please
his teacher and his mama, but he was afraid to come all the
way into the water.

"Try again. I'll count to three, then you jump, and I'll
catch you!"

Our mommy-and-me swim lessons were off to a great start so far. I was going into my ninth month of pregnancy with my daughter and struggled to stay upright. If I could handle keeping my balance in an Olympic sized pool full of children, surely our son could at least come into the water. It's not that he was resistant to pools, it's that he didn't have his water wings. He was simply afraid.

After a little more coaxing, he finally threw one leg out and leaned in. Only, he didn't jump up and out. As soon as his momentum began to pull him to the water, he quickly twisted his body, and grabbed hold of the side of the pool.

He was in, he just wasn't *all* in.

How often do we do this?

We want to go back to school or go after a new job but there's no safety net.

Perhaps we have a dream that has been nagging at us for so long that it is beginning to seem impossible.

We want to lean in to our faith a little harder, but we're afraid of where that may lead.

We look down and stare at our toes, right on the edge of the line. We see the sweat drip from our brow down to our feet. In our peripheral vision, we see others who have taken the leap. They're jumping and smiling and are in their element. They don't even look back at the side of the pool anymore because the good stuff is found out in the deep.

Maybe we've taken a *half* leap into that next step, and we are suffering for it. Things don't go as we think they should, so we question what we are doing. We're sore, feeling beat up as we stick our toe into our future, only to pull it back at the first hint of discomfort. We're tired because we have half of our time spent on moving forward while our other half is spent in the comfortable.

This is when we have to make some decisions.

He is beckoning us to trust Him.

Completely.

He's asking, *"Are you all in?"*

Am I?

Are we?

After a few of these leans into the water, my sons's little fingertips began to feel raw from the concrete pool edge. He was getting winded as he would jump in and immediately swing his leg up on the edge to pull himself right back out. There was no fun in it. He wanted more.

Don't we want more?

You know how this ends. Once he finally took a real, genuine leap into the pool, he realized there was nothing to fear. I was always within arm's reach. His teacher kept his focus on her eyes as she instructed. He felt secure. Safe. He knew he could spread his arms and extend his legs and experience the freedom that a swimmer has. All without the fear of sinking.

When Jesus called His disciples, they dropped what they were doing and followed the call. Luke 5 tells us that Simon, James, and John literally pulled their boats out of the water and left them behind. No looking back.

Christ gave His all for you and for me. He didn't turn around and grab hold of the edge when his Father called him to lay down his life for us. He trusted that his Father's plan was the perfect plan, and He kept his eyes on Him while constantly moving forward.

Because Christ gave His all, I believe He calls us to do the same. An even exchange. When we experience unrest in our spiritual lives and have difficulty leaving the ledge, perhaps it's because we want everything He has for us, while we only hand him a portion of ourselves. It's in handing him only pieces of ourselves that we can begin to feel pulled apart.

If Jesus is calling us out, we need to be all in.

That job. That dream. That life of faith.

Let's leave the ledge. Leap out. Let go.

Even if we do it scared. We can't go wrong. He won't let us sink.

Lord,

Thank you for loving us right where we are, and also for loving us too much to let us stay there. Help us to stay focused on you as you lead us to strengthen our faith and love you more. Help us to jump big and to be all in.

In Jesus' name,
Amen

Day 2 Reflection

CREATED TO BE, NOT TO DO

It's not about you.

We love to talk about our issues, our challenges, our past... but for now, we are exploring why we were created in the first place.

Let's talk about *love*.

Before I even get started, I bet I can read your mind. You're already thinking that I'm going to tell you that you were created to love others. That we are here to lavish love onto those who are less fortunate and to give of ourselves until we are empty. That in loving others, we will find our purpose.

Wrong. And right.

Today we aren't talking about our performance.

We are talking about *being* loved.

Love
One of the most overused words in the English language.
One of the most weighted words in the English language.
One of the most desired titles in the English language.

Why a title?

Don't we all want to be loved? To be cared for and thought of? Don't we all long to have someone who is wise, caring, discerning, someone who keeps our best interest in mind, who is fair and gentle to love us?

I say yes.

Look around.

Movies are always centered around a relationship where either love conquers all or someone is looking to be loved.

Authors make millions of dollars selling books telling stories of two people not meant to be together who find their way through every roadblock until they intersect in the last chapter and live happily ever after.

Women young and old let things go too far too quick in dating relationships hoping they will be loved in return.

Our culture is inundated with stories and photos and music that awaken something deep within us that says, "Somebody love me!"

Where do we think this desire to be loved comes from?

Why are we wired this way?

God
He placed in each of us the desire to be loved. *He* did that.

Why?

Because He wants to be the one to fulfill that longing. He wants for me and for you to open our hearts up to Him to fill that hole.

How blessed is God! And what a blessing he is! He's the Father of our Master, Jesus Christ, and takes us to the high places of blessing in him. Long before he laid down earth's foundations, he had us in mind, had settled on us as the focus of his love, to be made whole and holy by his love. Long, long ago he decided to adopt us into his family through Jesus Christ. (What pleasure he took in planning this!) He wanted us to enter into the celebration of his lavish gift-giving by the hand of his beloved Son.

Ephesians 1:3–6 The Message

Read this again. Read it slowly.

"...*long before the earth's foundations*..." He envisioned us.

"...*he had us in mind*..." He thought of us.

"...*settled on us as the focus of his love*..." He chose to make us his center.

"...*adopt us into his family*..." Before we were born, He knew He wanted us.

"...*He wanted us*..." His mind was made up.

"...*his lavish gift-giving*..." He planned to demonstrate His love for us.

None of this has anything to do with our performance. None of it.

One of the reasons you are here on this earth is for God's pleasure.

So He can love you.

He takes pleasure in loving you!
It you are a parent, think of it this way. Don't you love your children just the way they are? Don't you cherish the fact that you have this child and that they are yours. They carry your name. They resemble you in appearance.

What if they were lying in a hospital bed and were unable to do their chores. Would you love them the same as when they could hold a broom?

What if they got caught up in the wrong crowd and went astray for a while. Would you love them the same as when they were under your wings?

What if they lived their lives pursuing their dreams. Would you love them any less if they did not?

That parental love...it's not performance based. It doesn't come with conditions.

I John 4:8 tells us that "God *is* love." It's His nature. His character. We were created in His image and that love resides in us. Both our desire to love and our desire to *be* loved.

Let's settle on this for now...*you exist so that God can love you.*

He loves you whether you want it or not.

He loves you whether you think you deserve it or not.

He loves you whether you are walking in His ways or not.

He loves you. Period.

Like a loving father, even if you push back, run away, or turn your back on Him, He still loves you.

He has since before the foundations of the earth were set.

So let's rest in that. Breath it in. Believe it.

Lord,

At times, I feel unlovable. Help me to accept your love for me no matter how I'm feeling. Thank you for this free gift.

In Jesus' name,
Amen

Day 3 Reflection

BE KIND TO YOURSELF

Jesus told a lot of stories using agricultural references to make His points so that people could easily relate.

He talked about soil.
He talked about planting seeds.
He talked about watering.
He talked about being rooted.
He talked about pruning.
He talked about harvesting.

We talk a lot about planting seeds into the lives of *other* people. The words we use, the actions we take to show how we really feel about someone or what we think they're worth.

Have you ever given thought to what we plant into our own lives?

Do we scatter healthy thoughts like these into ourselves?

- Words of bravery and strength whispered under our breath when we feel weak.
- Taking time to care for and love ourselves ... spending time alone or with friends, getting that pedicure, lifting those weights, reading a good book, getting good sleep.
- Are we quick to forgive ourselves when we mess things up, extending the same grace to ourselves that we would give to our loved ones?
- Seeds of "You can do this!"?
- Words of kindness when we look in the mirror and don't like what we see...words like "beautiful," "able," "strong," "work in progress," and "capable."

Or

- Do we punish ourselves with words like "what's wrong with me?"
- Do we dwell on the past and let it stunt our spiritual growth?
- Have we let seeds of bitterness take root and contaminate the soil of our soul?
- Do we look in the mirror or at the scale and chastise ourselves (this is sometimes me) for enjoying an ice cream with our child?

We have to be intentional with what we plant in our hearts. If the Holy Spirit lives there, He deserves the best, and He only wants the best for you and me.

I have this on my bulletin board in my office: "If you wouldn't say it to a friend, don't say it to yourself."

When my work is going slow or my pants are feeling too tight or I've blown it with one of my children or I'm wrecked with worry over a situation I can't control...I try to plant good seeds into my own soil.

We have to be intentional.
Storms will come and force us to react. Let's protect the good seeds we've planted. Fight for them. Let's not allow our temporary circumstances to rip our seeds of truth from the soil of our souls.

People will come and try to trample on that which we've planted. We can post a "no trespassing" sign.

Drought will creep in. Let's recognize it quickly and reach back for the living water which is God's word.

Bad seed can be thrown on us by others. It can take root before we've realized it's there. Get out the hoe and get that out before its roots go too deep!

We have to be patient with ourselves.
Sometimes some dreams some desperate prayers, they need to work underground before they can burst forth.

A wounded heart may take some time before it is healed.

Bad self-esteem can steer us wrong more times than we'd like to admit before that seed has been removed.

The soil of our heart may need tending to. Ten good seeds for every one bad.

We have to be hopeful.

We have a Master Gardner who knows exactly when those seeds will sprout. He tells us in His word how to care for what has been planted inside of us.

He won't let any good seed go to waste, we can count on that.

His words are the good seed. We can't rely on people for this. Our worth, our purpose, our courage, it all comes from Him. All of it.

My word that goes out from my mouth:
It will not return to me empty,
but will accomplish what I desire
and achieve the purpose for which I sent it.

Isaiah 55:11

That which has been planted through the leading of the Word *will* eventually bloom. It *will* eventually show itself. And, it *will* be good.

Incredibly good.

So, let's be kind to ourselves. Let's remind each other to be kind to ourselves. Let's remember whose we are and that He thinks the world of us. We don't like seeing our own children beating themselves up when they're feeling a little low, so let's not do it to ourselves.

> *We are children of The Most High, daughters of*
> *the King chosen before the beginning of time to come*
> *into the family of God!*

Let that sink in.

Lord,

We live in a time when it's easier to compare ourselves to others than to take you at your word. Forgive me when I meditate more on others' opinions of me more than who you say I am. Help me recognize when I need to get out the hoe and remove anything planted in my heart that will keep me from you. Thank you for loving me just as I am.

In Jesus' name,
Amen

Day 4 Reflection

KEEP IT SIMPLE SISTER

I don't know about you, but my mind can get so consumed with life that it affects me negatively. Even if most of my thoughts are positive, they can be all consuming. Overthinking can cause me to doubt my abilities, worry about things that are completely out of my control, and physically drain my energy. When my mental energy is sapped up by too many thoughts, it can make me physically exhausted and spiritually weak.

But I'm working on that.

Our thought life sets the attitude and direction of our *spiritual* and *physical* lives.

When we are consumed with concerns and worry, it can take a toll on our *physical* bodies. Our eyelids tend to get heavy earlier in the evening. Our muscles can ache. Headaches will come and go. We may turn to food or cigarettes or pills or some other vice to look for relief from the pressure that has built in our minds, even if it is temporary.

When we are consumed with concerns and worry, it can take a toll on our *spiritual* life. If we haven't made reading the Bible and prayer a discipline in our daily lives, it's easy to just skip it. Or, we read a Bible verse and immediately think "so and so sure could benefit from that one!" rather than ourselves. We can doubt our faith. Doubt our God. We might even gravitate toward others whose minds run a mile a minute as well and we can commiserate together instead of praying for one another.

> *But seek first his kingdom and his righteousness,*
> *and all these things will be given to you as well.*
> *Therefore do not worry about tomorrow, for*
> *tomorrow will worry about itself. Each day has*
> *enough trouble of its own.*

Matthew 6:33–34

This is so simple.

If you've ever wondered what God's will is for your life, here ya go! Yes, there is more to it than just this...but this is where our focus should be. He tells us clearly that if we seek Him out, the other things in our lives will be given to us. They will fall into place as they are meant to. He will take care of the details. He says not to worry about tomorrow. Don't worry about it. Don't.

I know this is much easier to read or say than to apply. Like I said, I'm working on it too. The struggle is real. But we must make the effort. We've got to keep our eyes on Him...not just because He says so, but because there's a blessing that comes when we do.

His kingdom...the family of God.

kingdom

noun king·dom \ˈkiŋ-dəm\
Definition of *kingdom*
: the eternal kingship of God
: the realm in which God's will is fulfilled

His righteousness...His character.

righteous

adjective righ·teous \ˈrī-chəs\
Definition of *righteous*
: morally good : following religious or moral laws
: acting in accord with divine or moral law : free from guilt
    or sin

I want less stress. I want less worry. I want less wondering about what tomorrow will bring. I want more peace, more confidence, and more freedom in my mind.

Am I the only one?

When we are feeling consumed by our circumstances, remember the K.I.S.S. method.

Keep
It
Simple
Sister

Take things one day at a time. Focus on Him. His leading. Trust Him.

The more I study and write and live, the more I feel He is asking me over and over, "Do you trust me?" I'm trying to stay focused on Him and let Him take care of my tomorrow. After all, I don't know what is coming, but He does.

What is it in your own life that you need to hand over to Him in exchange for keeping your focus on who He is? One thing for sure is that your worrying will do nothing to change it. Not one thing.

I have my one thing for today that I'm handing back over to Him. Won't you join me with your own stuff? He tells us if we do, that "all these things will be given to you as well."

It's really all about trusting Him.

Trust in the Lord with all your heart and lean not on your own understanding; in all your ways submit to him, and he will make your paths straight.

Proverbs 3:5–6

Seek.
Trust.
It's so simple.

Lord,

Thank you for your instruction. For its consistency and constant guidance to put you first in all things and trust you with the rest. Help me when I need a re set to get back to this simple structure found in your Word.

In Jesus' name,
Amen

Day **5** Reflection

THE CHOICE IS YOURS

*"I have the right to do anything," you say—but
not everything is beneficial. "I have the right to do
anything"—but not everything is constructive.*

I Corinthians 10:23

When my children were really small, they *had* to do whatever in the world I told them too. Get in the car. Get in the bath. Stay out of the refrigerator. Bring me your book bag.

There came a time when one of my sweet children (who shall remain nameless) began asking me after my directions, "What will you do to me if I *don't* do that?"

What?

This child was weighing out the consequences. They were deciding whether it would be worth the adventure to just flat out do it their own way and take the punishment rather than obey and keep peace in our little family.

The reality is, that child could choose not to get in the car, get in the bath, stay out of the fridge, or bring me said book bag.

It was their choice. They had the freedom to choose in those moments.

I wasn't delving out instructions because they needed to know who was boss. I didn't take pleasure in pointing my finger with "go here" and "sit there" and "do it now."

Everything I told my kids to do was in their *best interest*. Whether short term or long term, it was to their advantage to just obey.

Loading up in the car was the pathway to school or Mimi's house, a bath kept them clean, unnecessary trips to the fridge would spoil their dinner and there were things in the book bag I was expected to sign and initial or else my children would suffer consequences the next day from their teacher.

You see, it wasn't always about right and wrong and being bossed around, it was about knowing what was best for them and keeping them on the right track. A track that would ultimately be for their good.

Today we have laws and rules and convictions we are told to follow, but like our children, we are tempted to do things our own way.

We like to question.

But there is an authority who knows what's in our best interest and we'd be wise to listen to Him.

Incredibly wise.

No temptation has overtaken you except what is common to mankind. And God is faithful; he will not let you be tempted beyond what you can bear. But when you are tempted, he will also provide a way out so that you can endure it.

I Corinthians 10:13

Whenever we are tempted to take action that contradicts with His word, He helps us flee from that temptation. That is great news! Temptation is going to be a part of life. He calls us to lean into Him during those times and ask Him how to escape that thing. Whatever it is.

Here's what I know, the directions He gives to us are for our benefit. It's not to restrain us from becoming the "real us," it's to keep us away from the things that will keep us from becoming who we were made to be. We are His creation. He knows what's best for us. He knows what's coming around the corner of our lives. He knows how we need to be prepared best.

But alas...

I'm free to stand on railroad tracks.

I'm free to drive at high speeds.

I'm free to walk across a busy highway without looking both ways.

I'm free to view pornography.

I'm free to charge up my credit cards.

I'm free to gossip.

I'm free to yell at my husband and children when I'm angry.

I'm free to ignore the Holy Spirit when it nudges me to do something.

I'm free to stay away from church.

I'm free to cheat on my spouse.

I'm free to lie to my boss.

What is it in God's word that you struggle with the most?

What if we stopped looking at God's book as a rule book and instead looked at it as a play book?

Like a coach teaching and training their team, when the players execute the plays as they've been taught, more ground is gained and the coach is pleased. The team is heading in the right direction.

Doing things God's way won't come without obstacles and challenges, but it will produce more wins than losses.

He gives us the freedom to make our choices, just like my children had freedom. But the consequences are never worth the rebellion.

I've heard the Bible referred to as a "book of instructions" or an "owner's manual for life" and those labels have some significance to them. But the difference in using the book as just a manual or instruction book and reading it for it's overall purpose is very different.

The One who wrote *the* book...He *is* the book.

In the beginning was the Word, and the Word was with God, and the Word was God.

John 1:1

When we read and study the Bible, the best part of our learning isn't in the rules or commands, it isn't in the answers we're looking for or the list of dos and don'ts we may find.

It's in those pages that we see who God really is. How He loves us. His character. His heart. What motivates Him when He teaches those commands.

Mamas have their children's best interest in mind when they teach them.

Coaches have their team's best interest in mind when they instruct them.

God has our best interest in mind when He gives us wisdom through His word to help us make wise choices.

We make our own choices but then our choices make us.

Let's be careful. Let's be teachable.

Let's be grateful for the freedom to choose and the knowledge that the One who helps us to make our choices does so out of love.

Lord,

Thank you for the freedom of choice. What a great and glorious gift it is. Today, I choose to love you first and my neighbor as myself. I choose to shift anything in my life that is keeping me from doing that. I ask for your help and thank you in advance for the freedom that is found when I do things your way.

In Jesus' name,
Amen

FRAME It!

1. As we moved our relationship with Christ up to the very top of our priority list over the last thirty days, take stock of what had been placed ahead of your relationship with Him until now and jot those down here. These could be other people, your work, hobbies or _____ (fill in the blank).

2. Scripture tells us that those things listed above will work themselves out for your good when you love God:

   And we know that in all things God works for the good of those who love him.

   Romans 8:28

   How does this encourage you?

3. Our love for others develops and deepens over time as get to know one another more intimately. Think of some ways you can begin to implement growing your relationship with Christ and jot them down here. These might include daily reading of the Bible, spending time with other believers and

asking them about their faith journey or something as simple as starting a gratitude journal.

4. What are your biggest take aways from your journey to a simpler faith?

THE WRAP-UP

I hope if you felt as if your faith in Christ looked more like a wadded-up ball of yarn than a straight line to His heart, you feel a bit untangled now.

I hope if you were ever told to put your good deeds ahead of your one-on-one relationship with Christ, you understand now you were taught falsely.

I hope the last four weeks has felt like a breath of fresh air that is full of confidence that Christ loves you unconditionally.

I hope you give yourself a moment to reflect and meditate on the truths shared here and the reaction your soul has had to each nugget.

Friends, loving God and loving others is a simple concept indeed, but it is the most necessary component to living the contented, joy-filled life we have been offered. Sometimes as women, over thinking comes more naturally than reading something in black and white and carrying on. As each new day appears before you, ask yourself, "How can I love God best and how will my relationship with Him cause me to love people today?"

Let us remember the conversation in Matthew:

> *"Teacher, which is the greatest commandment in the Law?"*
> *Jesus replied: "Love the Lord your God with all your heart and with all your soul and with all your mind. This is the first and greatest commandment. And the second is like it: Love your neighbor as yourself."*

Matthew 22:36–39

Jesus is so specific here and I love it! To love Him with our heart, soul and mind means we need to be attentive to all aspects of our being. How can we simply make up our minds to love God but not connect that decision with our hearts? How can our souls respond to His love for us and yet our minds tell our mouths to speak in opposition to what we know? It's all connected and it's up to us to make sure we are loving Him with our whole self.

And let's not forget that we cannot love our neighbor as ourselves if we don't first love God.

Without experiencing the relationship Christ wants with us, it is nearly impossible to truly love others. This is something that took me years to understand and frankly, I cannot apologize for it. Relationships take time and effort, and my faith walk has been steady, but at times, slow.

If you find yourself struggling to love others with the same, unconditional love He has for you, take it back to Him. Dig in the Word. Confide in a friend who does this well. And don't give up!

When we desire to follow God's lead, He will help us find our way. Because ultimately, He wants us close to Him. And following after Christ will always lead us in the way He desires us to go.

Yes, detours, speed bumps and natural disasters may slow us down or discourage us from time to time, but there is nothing that can keep us from growing closer to Christ permanently.

I don't know you, but I've been praying for you for a very long time.

If you aren't sure that you have a relationship with Jesus Christ, you can start today. And if you made this commitment to Him in the past and fear you have somehow severed your ties to Him, I encourage you to pray this prayer:

Lord,

Perhaps I've been deceived that religion is the same as a relationship with you. And that's what I want, a relationship.

I believe you sent your son Jesus to live and teach us and ultimately, pay the penalty for my sin by His death on the cross. I believe He rose again three days later and is now sitting

*in heaven with you. I want to make you first in my life. I'm
thankful for your love for me and I want you to be my Lord.
I love you. Thank you.*

In Jesus' name,

Amen

A fresh start. He's all about it.

If you prayed this prayer for the first time, or made
a recommitment to your faith in Christ, I would love to
know about it. More importantly, I encourage you to tell
someone you know. Someone who could encourage you to
spend time getting to know Jesus.

You are so loved! At the end of the day, let's ask ourselves if we loved God and people well and give ourselves
the grace to start fresh each morning. Not because it de-
pends on us, but because He's already showered us in it.

A fresh start.

A renewed love.

A simple faith.

I continue to pray that we all take deep, slow breaths,
and meditate on these truths.

|